WILD ITALY
Giulio Ielardi

Cover photographs:
front European Lanner *Falco biarmicus feldeggii*,
one of italian wildife treasures;
back cover little waterfalls at Foreste Casentinesi
National Park.
Ph. Giulio Ielardi

© 2011 Giulio Ielardi
All rights reserved
ISBN 978-1-4477-8268-1

Italian/English translation
Arabella Rodriguez

Website of the Author
www.giulioielardi.com

Contents

Foreword   7

1. ANIMALS

Valle d'Aosta / Gran Paradiso National Park
THE ALPINE IBEX   *11*

Lombardia / Stelvio National Park
GOLDEN EAGLE   *15*

Emilia-Romagna / Torrile Nature Reserve
HERONS AND OTHER MARSH BIRDS   *19*

Emilia-Romagna / Taro Regional Park
STONE CURLEW   *22*

Tuscany / Monte Labbro
MONTAGU'S HARRIER   *26*

Tuscany / Rocconi Nature Reserve
LANNER   *29*

Tuscany / Maremma Regional Park
RED FOX   *32*

Lazio / Tolfa Hills
MEDITERRANEAN BLACK WIDOW   *35*

Lazio / Simbruini Mountain Regional Park
WHITE-CLAWED CRAYFISH   *38*

Lazio / Rome
STARLING   *41*

Lazio / Duchessa Mountains Regional Reserve
GRIFFON VULTURE   *44*

Lazio / Valle delle Cannuccete Nature Monument
THE SPECTACLED SALAMANDER   *48*

Abruzzo / Abruzzo, Lazio, Molise National Park
APENNINE CHAMOIS   *51*

Abruzzo / Abruzzo, Lazio, Molise National Park
BROWN BEAR   *54*

Basilicata / Matera
LESSER KESTREL   *57*

2. LANDSCAPES

Piedmont / Alpi Marittime Regional Park
PIANO DEL VALASCO   *63*

Trentino-Alto Adige / Provincial Park of Paneveggio-Pale di San Martino
VAL VENEGIA   *66*

Trentino-Alto Adige / Adamello-Brenta Provincial Park
VAL DI GENOVA, HEART OF THE ALPS   *69*

Friuli-Venezia Giulia / Regional reserves of Valle Canal Novo and Foci dello Stella
MARANO LAGOON *72*

Liguria / Cinque Terre National Park
THE PATH OF LOVE *75*

Emilia-Romagna / Tuscan-Emilian Apennine National Park
THE MOUNTAIN OF DANTE *78*

Emilia-Romagna / Foreste Casentinesi, Falterona, Campigna National Park
THE ACQUACHETA WATERFALL *82*

Tuscany / Bolgheri Natural Reserve
THE TREASURY OF MAREMMA *85*

Lazio / Circeo National Park
THE ISLAND OF SEAGULLS *87*

Abruzzo / Gran Sasso and Monti della Laga National Park
THE ROOF OF THE APENNINE *90*

Campania / Cilento and Vallo di Diano National Park
SECRET CAMPANIA *93*

Sardinia / Gennargentu National Park
SUPRAMONTE COAST *96*

Sardinia / La Maddalena Archipelago National Park
CALA COTICCIO *99*

Sicily / Lampedusa Nature Reserve
THE TURTLE ISLAND *102*

Sicily / Alcantara Regional Park
THE GORGE OF THE VOLCANO   *105*

3. PLANTS

Lombardia / Palude Brabbia Nature Reserve
THE SECRET MARSH   *111*

Veneto / Dolomiti Bellunesi National Park
BUSA DELLE VETTE   *113*

Emilia-Romagna / Po Delta Regional Park
PUNTE ALBERETE FLOODED FOREST   *116*

Marche-Umbria / National Park of Monti Sibillini
THE RING OF THE VALLEY OF PILATO   *119*

Abruzzo / Majella National Park
THE FOREST OF SANT'ANTONIO   *123*

Puglia / Gargano National Park
MONTE SACRO   *126*

Basilicata / Pollino National Park
THE PINES OF THE "GRANDE PORTA"   *129*

Calabria / Sila National Park
IN THE GIANTS' SHADOW   *132*

Sicily / Etna Regional Park
BIRCHES ON THE VOLCANO   *136*

Sicily / Zingaro Nature Reserve
THE PATH OF THE PALMS   *139*

FOREWORD

This book comes with a purpose - to spread the word (I would like to say "tell the world", but modesty forbids) that the Italy of wildlife has little to envy that much better known Italy of art and history. That in short, not so far from the Colosseum, the Leaning Tower, the Grand Canal in Venice, are mountains and lakes and forests, offering the busy "Bel Paese" exciting encounters with the wilderness.
Even Italians know little about the wonderful natural environment of their country and are often unaware that the wolves and the bears are back in the Alps, the eagles and peregrine falcons are encouragingly on the increase, and chamois and deer inhabit forests and pastures in the Apennines.
The main cause of this welcome news is the creation of a network of parks established in Italy, especially in the last thirty years. Protected natural areas, large and small - number around 871, including 24 national parks and 134 regional parks - which with great difficulty not only protect the territory, but also achieve

environmental restoration, educational initiatives and promotion. This guide, however, does not just list the most important Italian natural resources. Rather it acts as a practical guide, providing concrete and detailed help to lead nature lovers, birdwatchers, photographers, to the right place at the right time.

It is divided into three chapters: the first is devoted to wildlife, the second to the landscapes, the third to the flora. Each is presented in geographical order from north to south, and each card is described by the of route to reach the different areas from the closest and most important cities (Rome, Florence, Venice, Naples, Turin etc.), almost all of which have their own airports.

Finally, in the following pages you will not find colour but B/W pictures: the reason lies in the need to keep down printing costs and to maximize the dissemination of the book. Interested parties are welcome, to fill the gap, the visit the website *www.giulioielardi.com*

Have a good trip through the Italy's wildlife.

Giulio Ielardi

1. ANIMALS

Giulio Ielardi

Valle d'Aosta / Gran Paradiso National Park

THE ALPINE IBEX

The "World's Most Beautiful Goat", as it has been defined, in Europe lives only on the Alps, and in Italy has its stronghold. Notably the species is distinguished by the long horns of the adult males, adorned with regular rings (the females have much less pronounced horns). Living at high altitudes, higher than the chamois, it uses its legendary ability to travel easily over rocks and look for herbs and lichens on which it feeds. In summer, females and young males enjoy life in herds. Winter is the mating season and the young, usually a pair, are born early the following summer. In the Gran Paradiso National Park there are now about 2600 ibex (*Capra ibex*). From here, over the last thirty years other groups have been introduced into several other Alpine areas such as Alpi Orobie in Lombardy, the Prealpi Carniche in Friuli, and the Alpe Veglia in Piedmont. In the park the best time for sightings is from May to October, when the alpine ibex graze the upper limit of the forest and meet in the early morning and evening. During the day they squat on ledges in the rocks, where they blend perfectly, and it is difficult to discern them.

Where
The Gran Paradiso National Park is the Alpine park par excellence, the first to be established in Italy in 1922. Its origin is really even earlier, dating back to 1856 when a game reserve was built to satisfy the desire of the Royal House of Savoy. Three years before the creation of the protected area, King Victor Emmanuel III gave properties to the Italian state that, after studying a commission created by the Minister of Agriculture, would become the centrepiece of the new national park, built "in order to preserve the fauna and flora and to preserve the special geological formations and the beauty of the landscape".

The mountains of the Gran Paradiso had in ages past been carved and shaped by large glaciers and streams that created the existing valleys, mainly the valley of Cogne, Valsavarenche, Rhemes side of the valley Valle d'Aosta, and the Orco Valley and Soana Valley on the Piedmont. Crops and human settlements cover a negligible area, more or less 4% of the park. Villages and pastures, often built of stone, tell the long history of civilization of the shepherds. Everything else consists of rocks, meadows, moraines and glaciers. The latter, both large and small, number over 60. The highest peak, the Gran Paradiso, reaches an altitude of 4,061m, and of the Alps is the only entirely Italian "four-thousander". Also present are numerous Alpine lakes, especially near the Nivolet hill, and some artificial basins on the Piedmont side.
Gran Paradiso National Park is reached by motorway A5 from Turin to Aosta. From Aosta follow the highway in the valley to Courmayeur, then after a dozen kilometers take the turning to Cogne.

The itinerary
The route starts from the village of Valnontey, easily accessible from Cogne. At the entrance of the village (altitude 1666 m) park the car, and with your backpack on yor back, follow the signs to the Sella refuge along the mule track. After the stream along the bottom of the valley you will soon reach the entrance to the Alpine Botanical Garden Paradisia, one of the most beautiful in the Alps. Almost all the natural environments of Alp mountains have been reconstructed here, and it even includes a garden of butterflies. Then you begin the gentle ascent through the conifer forest, sometimes following the route of the historic road built from 1865 onwards by King Vittorio Emanuele II, who wanted to be able to reach high altitude hunting grounds on horseback. You climb up out of the woods and here, on these first pastures, it is not difficult to spot the undoubted star of the park - that is the ibex. At the head of the valley you can also admire the vast glaciers of Gran Paradiso. To the right and left alternative routes signposted for Vernianaz and Grange Lauson meet and pass eachother. With one final leap, overcoming sharp bends, the trail overlooks the grassy plateau where the Rifugio Vittorio Sella rises at an altitude of 2,584m. Open from March to September, offers 150 beds as well as meals. Whoever wants to see the ibex must continue, however, leaving the shelter on the left and going as far as the head of the valley at 2,884m. The pastures of the Lauson with its eponymous small lakes, where the snow lingers until late in the season, are among the favorite for these animals and not infrequently you can watch marmots, chamois and the golden eagle hunting in flight (until here you walk about 3 hours). Please note: you could continue up the scenic Lauson Col (3296 m) and then go into Valsavarenche near Degioz-Eaux Rosses. Or, back to the Sella refuge, going back the way you came to the parking lot of Valnontey.

Giulio Ielardi

Internet
www.pngp.it

Lombardia / Stelvio National Park

GOLDEN EAGLE

A wingspan of over two metres and weighing three to six kilos, brown plumage with tawny head and neck, powerful black beak, yellow legs with well-developed claws. These are the classic characteristics of the golden eagle (*Aquila chrysaetos*), the best known and one of the most majestic birds of prey in Europe. The female is larger than the male, as is often found in birds of prey, while the young of the species are easily identified by three white spots on the ventral side of the wings and under tail. During their long vaulting flights patrolling an area of several hundred square kilometers, the wings are held in characteristic "V" position. They feed mainly on mammals, especially hares, marmots, wild rabbits and carrion but also some small chamois and roe deers, grouses and foxes. In Italy there seems to be a marked increase in numbers since the 70s, while bearing in mind today's more widespread network of detectors. On the Alps, the population density of breeding pairs (except for the erratic youngs, eagles are essentially sedentary) is close to optimal; while sadly in the Apennines, especially in the southern sector, many potentially good sites are not occupied due to poaching and habitat modification.

The latest estimate of the Italian population shows a total number equal to 486-547 pairs with 368-404 in the Alps. Italy has a great responsibility in the protection of this bird of prey: over 10% of the 4100-4500 nesting pairs in the European Union live in this country.

Where
Along the Alps, the Stelvio National Park is certainly one of the places with a higher population, and therefore more suited to observing these raptors.

Present in good number, it's no coincidence they were chosen as the very symbol of the park. Within the boundaries of the protected area and its immediately surroundings there are, in fact, currently 24 breeding pairs of which 12 in Lombardy, 8 in Alto Adige and 4 in Trentino. In the park, botanists have counted at least 1,200 species of larger plants and trees, 600 fungi and 1500 mosses and lichens. A good example of this multicoloured universe is offered by the Rezia botanical garden on the outskirts of Bormio. The forests are the habitat for most of the species of animals in the park. Squirrels live here, like Black and Grey-headed Woodpecker, capercaillies and sparrowhawks, nutcrackers and Tengmalm's Owls. The salamander inhabits moist recesses, and the glades and the surrounding alpine meadows are the environments of the adder (both the asp *Vipera aspis* and common European Adder *Vipera berus*). In the forest lives the most representative mammals of the park, the red deer, easy to observe (preferably at dawn or evening) from the valley to the highest altitudes. Roe deer, chamois and ibex (reintroduced in val Zebrù in 1968 with samples taken from the Gran Paradiso park) are the other ungulates present, guaranteeing plenty of excitement for hikers. Above the tree line, the scenario changes completely. Among mammals, this is the kingdom of the stoat, the mountain hare, and especially the marmot. Ponds host the rare alpine newt, as well as brown trout, chars and leeches. Among the birds are grouses, choughs, redstart and many other species including eagle owl, ptarmigan, rock partridge, dotterel, the latter more easily observable during the late summer migration (September) as they fly towards their wintering quarters. Finally, the golden eagle in the Stelvio park should not be confused with the bearded vulture. This great vulture has returned to nest in Italy once again after an international re-introduction project starting at the end of the last century. Currently, the bearded vulture nests exclusively in the Lombardy area of the park in the province of Sondrio, with 4 pairs.

The itinerary
The best known among the valleys of the park for the beauty of its landscape, the Zebrù valley is also worth a visit for the likely possibility of observing the golden eagle in flight. From Milan follow the main road No.36 to Lecco 36 - Colico, then continue on to ss.38 Sondrio - Tirano to Bormio. From here you reach the village of Madonna dei Monti, Valfurva, and leave the car at the area called Niblogo. Here the trail, actually a cart-track, will take you in around five hours' walk to the Refuge "V Alpini" at the base of Vedretta dello Zebrù, on the southern slopes of the summit. The route at this point offers two choices. The first is to go back the way you came, but an interesting alternative is the path that connects the Refuge "V Alpini" with Val Cedec through the Zebrù Pass, where it's well worthwhile to pause and enjoy the view over the ridge of "Tredici Cime" that spans from Mount Cevedale to Pizzo Tresero, overlooking the basin of the Forni

glacier. The observation of eagles is possible throughout the entire journey.

Internet
www.stelviopark.it
www.parks.it/parco.nazionale.stelvio/Eindex.php

Emilia-Romagna / Torrile Nature Reserve

HERONS AND OTHER MARSH BIRDS

With the growing number of nature reserves and parks in recent decades, Italy's marsh birds are now among the easiest representatives of wildlife to admire. Thanks to observation points equipped with slits and trenches, it is possible to look closely and photograph ducks and herons, as well as the numerous waders.
In Italy there are hundreds of wetlands, fifty of which have been recognized and included in the list of sites of international importance drawn up under the Ramsar Convention. These consist of marshes, swamps, bogs, and natural or artificial areas of water, including permanent or transitional areas of shallow sea water. The region where wetlands are more numerous is Emilia-Romagna, mainly thanks to the presence of the delta of the major Italian river, the Po. But due to the vastness of these areas, and their fragmentation, birdwatchers and nature photographers in particular may prefer a more isolated little wetland not far from the middle of the Po: the reserve of Torrile, result of a skilful work of bioengineering.

Where
Torrile Nature Reserve is located in Emilia Romagna. Take the A1 highway from Bologna to Parma, driving for about a hundred kilometers. To reach the reserve, which is also an oasis of LIPU, the Italian Bird Protection League, take the road n.343 from Parma to Colorno. Once you reach San Polo Torrile turn left and follow the directions to the Oasis LIPU Torrile. At your destination you can leave your car in the large parking lot. Torrile reserve is open from March to November. The winter months offer the greatest number of individual birds, while the

transitional seasons (spring and autumn) the greater variety of species. The oasis is open to the public all year round on Thursdays, Saturdays and Sundays (between 9-13 hrs and 14-18 hrs). Guided tours for school groups are possible on other days of the week, but they must be booked by tel / fax, no. 0521 810 606. The oasis is closed from December to February.

The itinerary
The visit starts on foot, through the gate and along the long clay paths (accessible for disabled users), leading to the observation huts. At Torrile there are eight, of which at least a couple are particularly suited to nature photography. From the entrance it is a short step to the new visitor centre, basically a tower that houses ticket office (a visit to the oasis costs 5 euro, free for LIPU members), teaching rooms and a rooftop terrace.

Here there is a choice: on the right, a path leads along the southern shore of a large body of water, in front of which are three observation points, one of which (called "Swarovski," named by the company that sponsored the reconstruction) is very large; going left, instead, a wooden walkway takes you to a duck centre and then runs along the left facing a second pond where there are four other huts. One of them, called "bunker", has two floors, the lower of which offers - with windows just 70-80 cm from the water's surface – the best perspective for nature photographers (the best light being in the morning). What will you be able to see in Torrile? A surprising amount of birds: especially herons, such as the grey and the purple heron, white egrets, night herons, squacco herons but also kingfishers, marsh harriers, geese, ducks and cormorants. In winter you can regularly meet the rare spotted eagle, while in spring and autumn rare species like black stork, osprey, the glossy ibis arrive at the oasis. In practice, this is one of the places where it's easy to portray wild animals in Italy. It's worth mentioning how the oasis was created, from the transformation - at the end of the eighties - of an expanse of fields planted with corn and beets, by digging ponds and forming small islands which were soon colonized by birds. The oasis is wheelchair accessible and the Province of Parma has provided the protected area with a scooter suitable for travelers with physical disabilities and sensory impairment.

Internet
www.lipu.it/oasi/oasidettaglio.asp?133

Emilia-Romagna / Taro Regional Park

STONE CURLEW

It arrives in spring, but few realize it. It frequents the more open and bare environments such as river shingles or stony and dry pastures, but you need binoculars, experience and a good dose of patience to see it. It is the size of a large pigeon and has long yellow legs, a yellow super-eye which gives it its Italian name "Big-Eye" and lays its eggs in a small depression between stones. This I the stone curlew (*Burhinus oedicnemus*), bird-artist of disguise. In Italy this species is migratory and breeds regularly, though occasionally wintering here. It occupies the breeding sites in April and usually lay its eggs in May, although it is not unheard of for a replacement to be incubated later.

Where
The populations of this species, generally declining due to habitat changes and lack of versatility of preferred habitat, in Italy consist of often disjointed nuclei. One of the most important is housed and protected within the boundaries of the regional park of Taro, in Emilia Romagna. This right-hand tributary of the Po, the Taro, flows not far from Parma through the high plains east from the Via Emilia to the village of Fornovo. The park is a green strip about 20 km long and three thousand hectares in size, rich in the wide open landscapes from the broad riverbed, up to a mile wide. The A15 motorway Parma-La Spezia, made with the same Taro gravel, forms the western border. Twisted branches, canals, and river islands characterize the bed, bordered by strips of vegetation that separate the fields. Temporary wetlands are created by secondary branches of the river, submerged during floods. After decades of indiscriminated removal of pebbles by several quarries, today's park regulations prohibits quarrying of the river and works are being carried out to recreate the environment in an attempt to heal the wounds inflicted on the landscape. Regarding botanical richness, the bed is an interesting but very inhospitable environment for most species. A few pioneer plants such as *Poligonum lapathifolium, Anthrisus caucalis, Cynoglossum creticum* can cope with the drastic alternation of prolonged droughts and floods. Where the pebbles are able to retain sand and clay, vegetation is enriched with other presences, most notably *Inula viscosa* and willows, able to withstand short periods of submergence during autumn floods: the territory of park hosts several species, including the most popular red willow *Salix purpurea, S. eleagnos, S. alba* and *S. triandra*. The driest areas of the river terraces are home to dense shrubbery with *Hippophae rhamnoides*, buckthorn *Rhamnus alaternus* and some of the 19 varieties of orchids catalogued by botanists within the boundaries of the protected area. Green frogs, common and green toads, tree frogs, great crested and common newts are among locally present

amphibians, while the reptiles include, among others, the European pond turtle, grass and dice snakes. South European nase, *Barbus* sp., *Leuciscus muticellus* and spined coach are among the fishes in the river, while the invertebrate species also include extreme rarities such as the beetle *Osmoderma eremita*. Among the mammals, besides the most common fox and hare, zoologists observed animals such as badger, skunk and weasel, the water shrew and the European water vole, and seven species of bats (including rare *Tatarida teniotis*). As for bird life, there are about 270 species that were observed, both those that remain all year round and breed or those that just visit occasionally , especially during migration. On the riverbank in particular, as well as stone curlew, other species of conservation priority nest here, such as the little tern and common tern.

The itinerary
To reach the Court of Giarola, a monastic complex of medieval origins now hosting the headquarters of the park, follow the A1 motorway from Bologna to Parma, then the A15 Parma - La Spezia exiting at either the Parma Ovest or Fornovo tolls. From Parma Ovest, continue towards Parma and, having crossed the river bridge, take the road right for Collecchio, then continue towards Fornovo and, at Pontescodogna village, turn right on to Strada Giarola. From Fornovo, continue towards Collecchio and Parma; after the village of Gaiano follow the signs to the Court of Giarola, which is located on the left. Along this 20 km stretch of river, on both sides but especially on the right, there are 10 equipped trails winding through the banks. Outside these paths, some of the areas of gravel in the heart of the park are subject to regulated access from April to August, to limit the disturbance to breeding birds: it is best to check before visiting the park at the Court of Giarola's visitor centre.

Internet
www.parcotaro.it
www.parks.it/parco.taro/Eindex.php

Tuscany / Monte Labbro

MONTAGU'S HARRIER

A ghost with wings hovers low over the fields, following the undulations of the earth. From time to time it gathers itself and dips suddenly in the tall grass, sometimes emerging with a vole or a lizard in its talons. More often the dive is in vain, and with a leap into the air it takes to the wing again, continuing its silent ambush, the sky full of little unsuspecting beings. Among european birds of prey, Montagu's harrier (*Circus pygargus*) is one of those whose sexual dimorphism is most present. Females have a camouflaged plumage with marked stripes on the wings, while males sport a more eye-catching dress contrasted with gray dorsal and black and white ventral plumage, with even black wing tips. The young resemble the females in the first year, but with a decidedly more reddish color. After a winter spent in Africa (during which the European Hen Harriers come in Italy, instead), Montagu's is present in the Italian and European skies from April to September. In the search for prey it mainly frequents arable or uncultivated fields, where they also lay their eggs in a nest on the ground. Evolution has developed protection against foxes and snakes; their eggs and chicks are often able to escape thanks to the dense ground cover area provided by scrupulous adults, but not against the tractors working in the fields every summer that unwittingly cause untold bloodshed. Pairs breed in usually sparse colonies, with breeding sites often a few hundred meters distant from eachother.

Where
In Italy, Montagu's Harrier reside mainly in the north-central regions, though they can also be found in Puglia and Sardinia. In many rural areas, such as those of Lazio (the province of Viterbo), the species is rapidly diminishing because of

environmental change and mechanized agriculture. In Tuscany, the most important area is that of Monte Labro (or Labbro), a relief of 1193 meters, which rises to the south-western edge of the famous Mount Amiata (of volcanic origin). The area is characterized by a very low urbanization and yet boasts a regional reserve. Fields and scattered farmhouses, forest edges, rocks, large areas of uncultivated land sometimes carpeted with ferns and patches of bramble offer to harriers an ideal habitat to feed and breed in peace. The same areas are inhabited by other birds of prey like short-toed eagle, lanner falcon, buzzard, honey buzzard, red kite recently re-introduced with a Life project (Monte Labbro is included in a Natura 2000 EU network area). Among other, significant local fauna present are the ortolan bunting *Emberiza hortulana*, the tawny pipit *Anthus campestris*, the rock thrush *Monticola saxatilis* and, among amphibians, the yellow-bellied toad *Bombina pachypus*.

The itinerary
The secret of the integrity of Mount Labbro, in the inland Maremma, is the absence of paved roads. However, there is a network of dirt roads that allows a good exploration of the area, of course, complete with hiking for a deeper understanding. This itinerary starts from Roccalbegna (in the province of Grosseto), but there are points of access from Arcidosso, Santa Fiora and Stribugliano. To reach Roccalbegna from Rome, follow the Via Aurelia (including the fast A12 motorway to Civitavecchia) to Grosseto South, then exit the Aurelia by following the signs for Istia of Ombrone and then Scansano. After a fuel station, turn left where the signs to Roccalbegna begin and follow them until you reach the village. After the village (situated in an idyllic position at the base of pinkish rock walls) follow the directions to Arcidosso. After about 3 km, about halfway towards the hamlet of Triana, is a turning on to a dirt road on the left-hand side, signposted to Mount Labbro and the Pescinello nature reserve, full of monumental trees. The climb, to be undertaken with caution due to the rough and rocky road, ends near the summit of the mount where the Giurisdavidic tower stands, the circular nineteenth-century monument built by the religious movement founded by the preacher David Lazzeretti (1834-1878). Further along the road descends towards the village of Santa Caterina, through vast uncultivated areas frequented by harriers. Take note: after the summit the road suddenly gets worse and anyone not equipped with an off-road car had better go back the way they came.

Internet
www.parks.it

Tuscany / Rocconi Nature Reserve

LANNER

It looks like a peregrine, but it is not. It's elusive like few others, rare and definitely one of most threatened raptors we have in Europe: it's the lanner falcon (*Falco biarmicus feldeggii*). Its main population is found in Italy, comprising about 140-172 pairs, the feldeggii is the lonely lanner of Western Paleartic. Known and described by emperor Federico II in his famous treatise "De arte venandi cum avibus", the lanner is now listed in the main international directives. There is also an Action Plan from BirdLife International for this bird. To recognize a lanner in the wild, and to distinguish it from more common peregrine *Falco peregrinus*, which is very similar in voice and size, is not easy. Among the characteristics visible in flight and from a distance, the most helpful distinction is the contrast between light flight-feathers and dark coverts of the underwing. The feathers of the nape are dark brown in female, brown in the male. The mustache is less pronounced than in the peregrine, compared with which the shape of the head has a much flatter top. This is a bird that remains throughout the year at the site where it breeds, on even modest cliffs of limestone, sandstone and tuff. They often hunt in pairs, plundering not only birds but also small sized mammals, catching them on the ground.

Where
The Italian region where lanners are more numerous is Sicily. In spite of environmental changes, poaching and - perhaps - competition with the peregrine (ornithologists are not agreed on this point), there are 80 - 100 nesting pairs on the island. Puglia and Basilicata host notable populations, while in central Italy there are a few localized pairs, Emilia Romagna being the northern limit. As in other regions (eg Lazio), Tuscany has

shown in recent years a further decrease of the species, in part for unknown reasons. Among the sites where the presence of lanner fortunately seems stable, thanks to careful surveillance and an unspoilt environment, was the regional reserve of Rocconi, managed by the WWF. But in 2011 late winter the male of local pair is suddenly disappeared, so the breeding saeson is blurred.

The reserve is located in southern Tuscany and covers about 371 hectares in the municipalities of Roccalbegna and Semproniano (province of Grosseto), along the river Albegna. Part of the protected area (130 ha) is owned by the WWF. Here landscapes are harsh and wild, and the Albegna river and its tributary Rigo have dug through spectacular limestone walls, interrupting a sequence of thick forests and pastures, hedgerows and patches of shrubs. A landscape of the past! Eight species of birds of prey nest here: in addition to the lanner we must add the peregrine and kestrel, sparrowhawk, buzzard, honey buzzard, short-toed eagle and goshawk. In effect, Rocconi is a pearl of a park not only in Tuscany but in Italy as a whole.

The itinerary
To go from Rome to Rocconi takes three hours. Follow the Via Aurelia (and suddenly the fastest highway A12 to Civitavecchia) to Grosseto South, then exit the Aurelia by following the signs for Istia d'Ombrone and Scansano. At a fuel station, turn left where the signs to Roccalbegna begin and follow them up until you reach the town. Visits to the Rocconi reserve must be accompanied by a guide and take place on Sunday by appointment, starting at 9 (tel. 347 5823441-0564 989 098). Updated information on the lanner and other treasures of Rocconi biodiversity can be obtained from Riccardo Nardi, naturalist and creator of the reserve (tel.346 8576803, riccardonardi@gmail.com), who in addition to Italian also speaks English and German.

Internet
www.wwf.it/rocconi.nt

Tuscany / Maremma Regional Park

RED FOX

It lives in almost any environment: deciduous and coniferous woods, grasslands, high altitude maquis, rural areas, wetlands, not disdaining even towns and suburbs of large cities. The red fox (*Vulpes vulpes*) is the most common carnivore in Europe and it is not difficult to observe it in the evening and at night while crossing roads or near towns. Of slim build, reddish-brown fur, ears erect and long snout, it is little more than half a meter long, but the bushy tail can almost double its size, bringing it to around 40 cm. This is a ubiquitous canine, present in Europe, Continental Asia (except the tundra), Japan, North Africa and North America. It was even introduced in Australia. In Italy it is widespread throughout the country, including Sicily and Sardinia.

Where
Although spotting this animal is not a rare experience, it's very easy and satisfying to view it in one of the beautiful protected areas of central Italy, along the Tuscan coast - the regional park of Maremma. Indeed here, as local nature photographers know very well, some surprisingly confident foxes have grown so accustomed to close contact with man as to be unafraid. The landscape of the park, which extends for 25 km along the coast on about 9000 hectares in the province of Grosseto, is characteristic of Tuscany, with *butteri* (local cowboys) and large herds of cattle raised in the wild. The landmark on this horizon is the green coastal ridge of the Uccellina mountains, actually hills little more than four hundred metres high, punctuated with the romantic ruins of old watchtowers and a medieval abbey. At their feet the Tyrrhenian sea stretches to the west, with pristine beaches and rocky shores, and to the north, the flat plain of the mouth of

the river Ombrone. In marshes teeming with life, monumental pine forests and solitary pastures, lives a rich fauna that includes among others crested porcupine and deer, fallow deer, and wild boar. There are many species of birds including peregrine and lanner falcon, harrier, hobby, wild goose, and stone curlew. For some years the park has been involved in a project to reintroduce the osprey, extinct for nearly fifty years in Italy (the last nest was occupied in 1968 in Sardinia). Several young falcons, collected in Corsica where there is a very vigorous population, were released locally after a period of acclimatization. They were also provided with artificial nests and shapes. Finally, in spring 2011, a pair nested in Maremma park and two chicks were born !

The itinerary
To get to Maremma park from Rome, follow the Via Aurelia (including a stretch of motorway A12 to Civitavecchia), to Alberese, just before Grosseto. From the town, to reach the site of

the park and visitors centre (we suggest a visit to obtain information and retrieve documentation), follow the signs first for Rispescia and then Marina di Alberese. The road makes a 90 ° bend through a farming village, and then points straight towards the sea, under a double row of pine trees. From here as far the parking lot behind the beach (where the road ends) you can see foxes in any direction, and which can be approached at any time of day by tourists traveling by car (for cyclists a bike path runs parallel to the road) as they search for easy food. Note, the access road to the Marina Alberese is controlled by a barrier - be prepared to pay a toll.

Internet
www.parco-maremma.it/index.php/en
www.parks.it/parco.maremma/Eindex.php

Lazio / Tolfa Hills

MEDITERRANEAN BLACK WIDOW

The mediterranean black widow (*Latrodectus tredecimguttatus*) is the Italian representative of a family spread throughout the world. Despite its bad reputation it is really quite a small arachnid. Measuring only up to 15 mm, the female is larger than the male, and has a bulbous abdomen and thin, hairless legs. The scientific name *Latrodectus tredecimguttatus* derives from the presence of thirteen red spots bordered by white found in the young. Its terrible reputation is due to its bite, definitely poisonous. Being quite a slow and not a very aggressive spider, a bite is fortunately quite rare. Among the most immediate symptoms is the onset of fever and nausea, and as more serious complications can follow, it is always recommend go to hospital. In Italy, however, the fatalities are very rare.

Where
In the Italian peninsula it is found in the southern and central regions, in the south of Tuscany and Liguria, preferring solitary stony Mediterranean environments such as low-lyng and degraded garrigue or maquis. Among the areas closest to Rome, it lives in the Tolfa hills, certainly the most interesting natural area near the Capital. These hills of low altitude, not exceeding 650 metres, are characterized by limited human activity. Few towns and few inhabitants. Few paved roads. Little rural development. Very few encounters along the dusty and bumpy dirt roads. The geological nature of the soil, of volcanic origin, together with the location near the coast and the climate, have created unique landscapes and biodiversity of great importance here, which is quite an attraction for scientists, naturalists, hikers and photographers. With regard to the vegetation, associations of species overlap in these hills, such as the typical Mediterranean

holm and cork oaks with the Atlantic species such as beech, *Ruscus aculeatus* and holly, and also with eastern Balkan species such as the Judas tree and eastern hornbeam. In all, the species number a thousand and include real treasures, such as the 40 or so species of orchid, including *Orchis papilionacea, O. morio, O. simia, O. apifera, Ophrys sphegodes*. The fauna is rich in variety but numerically poor, due to hunting. Most notable are birds of prey, with thirteen species present during the year, many of which nest here.

The itinerary
A road that cuts right through Tolfa hills starts from Allumiere. From Rome, take highway A12 to Civitavecchia as far as the exit for Civitavecchia Nord. From here follow the signs to Tolfa and Allumiere, but before you arrive in this last town, turn right for La Bianca. Fifty meters after this crossroads, turn right again on to a narrow road that first of all passes a few houses and then

proceeds for bend after bend through woods and pastures. After a few kilometers the tarmac ends at a clearing, where you can find a white fountain and the excavation of a Roman villa at the foot of Mount Tolfaccia. Here you go right - although the road becomes a dirt track, continue by car. After a descent and ascent, the road bends to the right under a high voltage pylon, actually a busy roost of red kites in the winter months. Go through another wooden gate (if closed, open and then close it) and you will reach another fountain: from now on, the ridge of pastures on the right (Poggio Freddara) is well populated by black widows. You can search for the sparse webs typical of the species in rocky areas, close to the ground and often including debris - be careful where you put your hands!

Internet
www.lifemontidellatolfa.it

Giulio Ielardi

Lazio / Simbruini Mountain Regional Park

WHITE-CLAWED CRAYFISH

This small freshwater crustacean (*Austropotamobius pallipes*), once widespread in rivers, is now increasingly rare both in Europe as a whole and the Italian peninsula in particular, and is classified as a threatened species (*vulnerable*) by the International Union for Nature Conservation (IUCN). Its main enemies are water pollution and non-native crayfishes - especially *Procambarus clarkii*, an american crayfish - which are formidable competitors but also carriers of disease. Its size is modest compared to those of its marine relatives. Larger than females, males can reach twelve inches in length and weigh in at 100g. Its preference is for small well-oxygenated streams with banks full of crevices where it can refuge during the day (being mainly noturnal) or in an emergency. Recently, the defining characteristics of the species *Austropotamobius pallipes* were reviewed and it is believed that the Italian crayfish, with the exception of those in the north-west of the country, belong to the species *A. italicus*.

Where
After the Alps, Lazio represents the region of Italy's richest waterways. But even here the impact of factors mentioned above have greatly reduced the numbers of crayfish in rivers and streams, and now in some rivers this crustacean is often found only in isolated groups. Behind Subiaco, in the heart of Lazio's Apennines, two thirds covered by woods, rise the mountains forming the largest protected area in the region: the natural park of Simbruini mountains, which extends over 29,990 hectares. Lush beech woods and karst plains are home to an important fauna, which includes animals like the golden eagle, the wolf and occasionaly the bear, owls, wild cats, red deers reintroduced recently. In the valley must also be added the art treasures

relating to the birth of the order of St. Benedict. Among the most important resources of the park are the water courses, starting with the Aniene - the main tributary of the Tiber River - which in the clear waters of its first section contains a fauna of great interest.

The itinerary
The main town of the district is Subiaco, from which our path begins. It is reached from Rome by the A24 motorway towards L'Aquila, exiting at Vicovaro-Mandela and then taking the state No.5 Tiburtina to the junction on the right for ss.411 Subiaco (75 km in total). From the town centre, follow the signs to the monasteries of St. Scolastica and the Sacro Speco but at the fork at the Roman Villa of Nerone, turn right on to a road which is at first paved before becoming a dirt track. We are now on the right bank of the lonely young Aniene, born on the slopes of Mount Tarino around Filettino village. Between meadows and groves of

beech, maple and walnut, frequented by squirrels, there is no shortage of pleasant opportunities to stop along the crystal-clear river. Crayfishes live into clear water of the river and of some puddles around the banks. The species, remember, is subject to absolute protection under Community legislation and with Italian laws.

Internet
www.simbruini.it/Eindex.php

Lazio / Rome

STARLING

Sturnus vulgaris itself. A bird common in Italy, indeed very common, easy to see in almost any environment excluding woods and mountain peaks. A successful passerine, with large ecological habits and gregarious behavior. It's a regular visitor to countryside, towns, cities. Its diet is of a broad spectrum, including insects, fruits, seeds, olives, cattle feed, all gathered on the ground or on vegetation. It does not build a true nest but lays eggs, beautiful light turquoise colored, using holes in tree trunks and branches, rocks or artificial cavities. City buildings, in fact, provide abundant shelter by way of roofs, cornices and gutters. In Italy some populations spend the summer in the north, migrating further south in winter, while in central Italy the population are believed to be at least partly stationary, although during the winter their numbers are added to with individuals from Northern Europe. In particular, from the end of September Italian cities begin come alive with the evening flights of starlings.

Where
Big cities host the most spectacular manifestation of this species, namely the large gatherings they form, particularly in winter, at dawn and dusk. The birds are attracted to the city by the higher temperatures cpmared to the country. Parks and tree-lined streets then become large collective roosts, causing some problems to traffic as their manure makes the asphalt slippery. The birds gather in the sky shortly after sunset. The flight of these massive groups of individuals, sometimes consisting of thousands of birds, leaves observers open-mouthed at the constantly changing forms that the flocks assume. However this is a sight that also draws fearsome predators like the peregrine falcon, who chases the flocks and attacks them with sudden dives. Then the black cloud

splits and frays, changing shape and wrapping itself in spirals in the air, looking sometimes like flying geometrical figures, or a heart, a dog bone, a butterfly, wherever form the imagination creates. Today, in Rome, where it began to nest in 1970, the starling is present on a massive scale and in some areas of the city during the winter months it is easy to see truly spectacular evening flights. A survey of about ten years ago counted at least 17 roosts in the Eternal City, for a total of several million individuals.

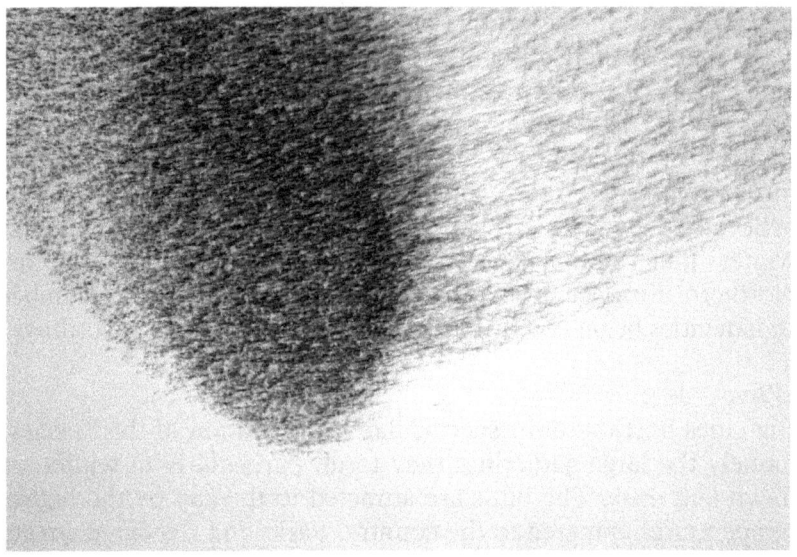

The itinerary
In the Capital there are several areas occupied by the starling's roosts, to the extent that in some cases the City Council has had to run for cover, because roosts in residential areas created traffic problems or public health risks because of the accumulation of droppings and feathers on the sidewalks, streets and parked cars. In particular, with the advice of LIPU (Italian League for Bird

Protection) measures were implemented to move roosts to parks and gardens. These interventions have been made through the use of the distress call, the call that bird normally issued in presence of danger, recorded and appropriately replayed near roosts they need to move. Currently there are two main areas to watch the evening gatherings during the winter months. The first is the large square in front of Termini Station, the main rail terminal in the city. Here, oaks scattered between the bus terminal, taxi rank and traffic lights provide a home to a large roost, thanks to the warmth generated by the powerful street lamps. Another and perhaps even better vantage point is located in the modern district of EUR, on the southern outskirts of the city. Extensive gardens around the artificial lake at the foot of the Sport Palace host the roost, and the wide view available offers the opportunity to enjoy the unhindered acrobatics of the flocks. There are also vantage points to be exploited like the nearby Palazzo della Civiltà del Lavoro. The underground stop EUR Palasport (B line) is exactly in the middle of the area described.

Internet
www.lipu.it/section/roma/storni.asp

Lazio / Duchessa Mountains Regional Reserve

GRIFFON VULTURE

The griffon vulture (*Gyps fulvus*) is one of the largest European birds, with a wingspan measuring up to 2.80 m. It lives in regions with great open pastures, steppes or grasslands where there are large herds of roaming cattle or large wildlife. It feeds exclusively on carrion, which it tracks with its highly acute vision during group flights. In Italy, until the 1990's it could be observed only in Sardinia; though in the coastal Northwest an important colony reinforced with specimens from Spain has existed for decades. In Sicily the species went extinct in 1965, and recently returned thanks to a reintroduction project operated by the Nebrodi and Madonie regional parks together with Lipu. In the Alps, the griffon vulture's return started in the spring of 1993, with the first verified eggs found on a cliff on the Friulian Alps. In the State Nature Reserve of Mount Velino, central Italy, a reintroduction project was initiated by the State Forestry Corps, again with specimens of Spanish origin. The first release of 1994 was followed by others, for a total of 59 birds between 1994 and 1997, which was when the first reproductions were recorded. Today, there are dozens of breeding pairs, and observations of the griffon have become commonplace.

Where
Among the areas frequented by vultures reintroduced in Abruzzo, the most spectacular is the wild valley of Tever, which separates the State Nature Reserve of Velino (now included in the broader Sirente-Velino Regional Park) from the regional reserve Montagne della Duchessa in Lazio. This is a protected area which covers an area just bordering Abruzzo near the A24 motorway. In the context of a typical Apennine landscape, it includes limestone reliefs incised by deep valleys, extensive high-

altitude grasslands and dense beech forests, surmounted high up by rocky ramparts resembling typical the Alpine scenery of Murolungo, Costone and Morrone. The jewel of the landscape is the small lake of the Duchessa, at 1788 meters, which occupies the bottom of a vast basin of glacial origin, subsequently shaped by karst, surrounded by meadows and pastures. The biodiversity is very rich. Of great interest, the fauna of the reserve includes all the best known and characteristic species of the central Appenine - with the exception of the chamois - including the wolf (estimated with one nucleus comprising a few members), roe deer, deer, eagle owl, golden eagle (nesting in neighboring Abruzzo), Orsini viper and, although found only sporadically, bear. One can frequently observe wild boar and, to a lesser extent, the squirrel. More difficult to spot are small mammals such as snow voles, garden dormouse, fat dormouse and shrews (*Sorex* sp.). Some reports also mention two other extremely elusive species such as the wild cat and the marten.

In the waters of lake lives a population of large but isolated great crested newt. Finally, one can also report the small group of collared parakeet that settled a few years ago in the village of Corvaro. Regarding the flora, well worth mentioning is the rare *Adonis distorta*, an endemic species with restricted distribution in small biotopes found at high altitudes (over 2000-2100 m) over the most imposing massifs of the Central Apennines (Gran Sasso, Majella, Sibillini, Sirente Velino). In the Lazio region it was only found on the summit of Montagne della Duchessa. From the fusiform rhizome with numerous lateral roots, prostrate or erect stems, the flower is isolated at the apex of branches with 8-18 yellow petals (rarely, white). It blooms between July and August on limestone gravel, at altitudes between 2,000 and 2,500 meters.

The itinerary
From Rome take the highway A24 to L'Aquila as far as the Valle del Salto toll. At the junction turn left towards Torano, taking particular care at a ninety degree bend to the right. In fact you need to take a dirt road that starts here, signposted to the nature reserve of Montagne della Duchessa, which leads to the most attractive access to the protected area - the tiny village of Cartore. After 4 km you reach the village, recently restored and perfectly situated at the edge of wide meadows. This is where the paths begin that allow you to visit the protected area. Those in the Fua and Cesa valley climb to the lake of the Duchessa, of glacial origin and that gave its name to the reserve, while that of the wild valley of Teve (well signposted) crosses the southeastern border in a particularly isolated setting. You walk for about two hours before leaving the forest, having first crossed a series of magnificent glades followed by high pastures until you reach Malopasso, from where, if you wish, you can go down to the lake of the Duchessa. As well as numerous griffon vultures, the golden eagle, peregrine falcon and lanner also frequent the area.

Internet
www.riservaduchessa.it

Lazio / Valle delle Cannuccete Nature Monument

THE SPECTACLED SALAMANDER

In the country of bear and wolf, this was chosen by Italian Zoologists Union as a symbol for their association (www.uzionlus.it). Across Europe it is found only in the Apennines; this little amphibian ten centimeters long is among the true stars of Italian fauna. It owes its name to the white spot that connects the eyes, while the rest of the back is blackish: in an emergency, the adult shows the bright red of the lower legs and tail, disorienting potential predators. Recent genetic studies have attributed to the Italian spectacled salamander two distinct species: the northern spectacled salamander (*Salamandra perspicillata*), from Liguria to northern Campania, and the southern spectacled salamander (*S. tergiditata*) from northern Campania to Aspromonte. Both species, nearly indistinguishable morphologically, live in fresh, clean running water and are difficult to observe during the day because they take refuge under rocks or leaf litter.

Where
The nature monument Valle delle Cannuccete is not far from the town of Palestrina, Lazio, and its famous Temple of Fortuna, site of one of the most popular oracles of Roman times. The small protected area - 20 hectares in size - includs a magnificent forest of big maples, oaks, hornbeam, saved from felling by a centuries-old rule designed to protect certain springs. These springs, by means of an aqueduct running partly underground, provided water for the ancient city of *Praeneste* (which gave its name to the local Prenestini mountains). The trunks of these great trees provide shelter to red and green woodpeckers, eurasian wryneck, nuthatch, tits and tawny and scops owls. A local story says that the musician Pierluigi da Palestrina, author of a famous *Stabat*

Mater, loved to stop under a huge oak, perhaps seven centuries old. Adjacent pastures host other species of birds and mammals as well as the squirrel and, in growing numbers as in the rest of Lazio, the crested porcupine. Today, thanks to the now isolated nature of these places, the wild cat and also of the wolf have recently been sighted. Le Cannuccete hold an important population of northern spectacled salamander (*Salamandra perspicillata*), reflecting the high environmental quality of the valley and the great importance of small protected areas for biodiversity protection. Also present are other amphibians including green and Apennine frogs (*Rana italica*).

The itinerary
From Rome, take the A1 motorway to Naples until the exit San Cesareo or stateway n.6 Casilina, then go towards Palestrina and Castel San Pietro Romano. Ignoring the ascending road to that town, follow the signs to Capranica Prenestina until the

signposted entrance on the right to Agriturismo Le Cannucceta. At the bottom of the road, from the restaurant's car park, go down to a little fishing lake, and on the opposite side take the path, climbing the gate: at the bottom of the next clearing, on the right, stands the oak of Pierluigi da Palestrina. Crossing the meadow you come down to the start of the forest, where a wooden gate just before the river (a board with a map of the area) indicates the start of a path that allows you to visit the protected area. The route is short though the journey time can vary greatly, depending on stops along the way. The search for the salamander, mainly active by night, is done with due care in the undergrowth litter or under stones and fallen logs. Given the very small size - about 10 cm long - and the darkness that surrounds a thick forest, it is not easy. The species, remember, is subject to absolute protection under Community legislation and with Italian laws.

Internet
www.parks.it/mn.valle.cannuccete/

Abruzzo / Abruzzo, Lazio, Molise National Park

APENNINE CHAMOIS

The Apennine chamois certainly is one of the more significant species of the Italian fauna. Long considered a subspecies of Alpine chamois, zoologists have today revised its endemic origins and have related it to the Pyrenees chamois, hence its scientific name is *Rupicapra pyrenaica ornata*. It is an ungulate of slender physique measuring up to 130 cm in length, to a shoulder height of nearly 80 cm. Present in both males and females and forming a hook, the horns are longer (up to 30 cm) compared to those of other chamois and the head has a mask of dark hair surrounding the eyes and reaching the muzzle. Threatened several times to extinction early last century, it was saved by the creation of Abruzzo national park in 1923 on an existing royal hunting reserve of the Savoy King. With the establishment in the early nineties of the other national parks of the Abruzzo Region – namely Gran Sasso-Laga and Majella - some nuclei of chamois were introduced there to reduce the risk of genetic inbreeding. Today the total Apennine population is about two thousand, half of whom live in the national park of Abruzzo.

Where
The national park of Abruzzo, Lazio and Molise remains the best place to observe the Apennine chamois in the wild. In particular, good visibility is ensured by a valley in the heart of the protected area: the val di Rose, which extends south of the village of Civitella Alfedena. In fact the stable presence of chamois in the summer months attracts thousands of hikers each year to the val di Rose, and the park authority has had to resort to limiting the numbers of entries to avoid excessive disturbance to the animals.

The itinerary
From Rome go to Civitella Alfedena, one of the main centers of the national park, via the highway A1 toward Naples as far as Ferentino. From here take the road to Sora and then follow signs for Pescasseroli (about 180 from Rome, calculate almost three hours of driving). At the junction of Opi, after the descent that follows the Forca d'Acero Pass, turn right towards Barrea and follow the road until the junction signposted for Civitella Alfedena. Civitella Alfedena is well known by tourists, especially for the area devoted to wolves, where some specimens have a large enclosure behind the last houses of the village. Climb the val di Rose, take the path marked J1 at beginning from the bottom - this is very uneven, and therefore uncomfortable. Beautiful views open up of Barrea lake, behind the village. Enter the beech forest that rises slowly, up to about 1700 m altitude where the forest ends and the landscape finally opens between Mount Sterpi d'Alto on the right and Mount Boccanera opposite.

With binoculars and camera handy, you can go back to this point at a leisurely pace keeping to the path - it is forbidden to leave it. Pastures and scree slopes continue through Passo Cavuto (1942 m). Hence the observation of the chamois is virtually guaranteed, given the stable presence of a pack fairly accustomed to hikers passing by. The passage is an excellent vantage point and if you want you can keep going for a few minutes as far as the refuge at Forca Resuni (1952 m). So far three-and-a-half hour walk. You can return the way you came, or take the parallel (and signposted) val Jannanghera, closing the loop at Civitella Alfedena (descent time two and a half hours). In summer these trails are limited and you should therefore book the excursion at the park offices a few days ahead.

Internet
www.parcoabruzzo.it
www.parks.it/parco.nazionale.abruzzo/Eindex.php

Giulio Ielardi

Abruzzo / Abruzzo, Lazio, Molise National Park

BROWN BEAR

This is the largest land mammal of the Italian fauna, and one of those most at risk of extinction. On the Italian Alps, a reintroduction project operated by the park Adamello-Brenta revitalised the local bear population, after it had been reduced to two or three individuals. Between 1999 and 2002 ten brown bears (animals taken in Slovenia, in cooperation with the local National Forest Service) were released in the Trentino mountains, where they have adapted, giving rise to a population which now consists of more than twenty specimens. But the largest group of Italian bears is to the south, in particular Abruzzo, and this one is special. The long isolation of the Apennine bears from his European neighbours has caused distinct genetic morphological characteristics (for example, being slightly smaller) and perhaps also behavioral modifications, according to zoologists - that make the subspecies Marsican Brown Bear (*Ursus arctos marsicanus*) absolutely peculiar to the mountains of the Italian peninsula. Currently a few dozen individuals are surviving, in a range centered on the National Park of Abruzzo, Lazio and Molise but extending to include the Apennines to the Sibillini, Simbruini-Ernici, Cicolano, Majella and others.

Where
Despite reports in several other areas of the Apennines, the core area of the presence of the marsican brown bear is located in Abruzzo and specifically in the historic national park, one of the oldest and best known protected areas in Italy. This is an area with large nuclei which are still wild, where more than eighty years of banning hunting and indiscriminate felling has allowed the preservation of a uniquely intact environment in an otherwise

crowded Italy. Wolf, Apennine chamois, deer, roe deer, golden eagle, goshawk, white-backed woodpecker, rock partridge, *Rosalia alpina* (among the largest and finest Italian beetles) are just some of the other animal species living in the park, largely covered by lush beech. Abruzzo's bears have an almost exclusively vegetarian diet and avoid man. Sightings are of course always possible, but it takes a bit of luck, and for many enthusiastic visitors to these mountains, lying face to face with a bear remains the unfulfilled dream of a lifetime.

But there is a time of year, between mid-August and late September, where bears frequent the summits of some of the mountains of the park, attracted by *Rhamnus alpinus* bushes, whose berries ripen at this time. Bears are greedy for their high nutritional value in preparation for the long winter hibernation. Taking the necessary precautions you can catch a glipse of bears at this time and in those areas - following the rules of the park – which considerably increases your chances.

The itinerary
From Rome head to Pescasseroli, taking the A1 motorway towards Naples as far as Ferentino. From here take the dual carriageway/main road to Sora, then follow signs for Pescasseroli (about 180 from Rome, allow for almost three hours of driving). From Pescasseroli (1167 m) follow the paved road to the ski lift of the Costa delle Vitelle as far as a signposted access to the park, last chance to leave the car. From here follow the path B1, which climbs in the beech forest of the valley Peschio di Jorio. The forest continues almost to the ridge, climbing steadily but without too much strain you come out just ahead of the Balzo dei Tre Confini. The track cuts some screes into the hillside colonized by *Rhamnus*, then rears up to reach the limestone bastion where - in an exceptional panoramic position - the refuge di Jorio is situated (1839 m, slightly less than two hours from the start). Warning: the ridge beyond the refuge is out of bounds during the fruiting of the *Rhamnus*, at risk of heavy penalties by the ever-present rangers. Return the way you came will take about an hour. For observations of bears, the best time is late in the day. It a good idea to participate in one of the frequent guided tours organized by local tourist agencies, which sometimes also include an overnight stay in the refuge.

Internet
www.parcoabruzzo.it

Basilicata / Matera

LESSER KESTREL

Like the bear and the wolf, this is one of the big stars of the Italian fauna, but most people do not know its habits, rarity, or even its name. Few know it, but the lesser kestrel (*Falco naumanni*) is among rarest European species of birds of prey, falling into the category SPEC 1 - that of greatest importance for conservation - by BirdLife. All the more unexpected, given its strong - if not exclusive - preference for the urban areas of mainland Italy where it chooses to reproduce. Eaves of churches and apartment blocks, gutters, often simply the spaces between the tiles of the old roofs, are chosen by the female to lay eggs, with yellow-orange spots and usually 3-5 in number. In Murgia di Bari and Murgia di Matera can be found one of the most important populations of lesser kestrel, distributed between Europe, North Africa, Turkey and West Asia. The preferred habitat for foraging for food - insects such as beetles, grasshoppers and crickets - is the pseudo-steppe, increasingly threatened - according to researchers - by the sprawl of modern suburbs, clearing fields of stones in order to plant new crops, and insensitive renovations in old towns.

Where
The best place to watch the lesser kestrel is the city of Matera, or rather its historical center. "Città dei Sassi" famous the world over, Matera is one of the most beautiful cities of Italy frequented by tourists, but not everyone knows that its oldest houses host hundreds of pairs of this rare little bird of prey. The Sassi are houses dug into the rock, until a few decades ago, by the families of poor peasants who could not afford a real house built of masonry: after careful restoration under UNESCO's the spotlight, these are now bed & breakfasts, shops and artists' studios, and a

few thousand people live there permanently. The city is part of a vast natural park of just over six thousand acres, the natural historic and archaeological park of Murgia, which extends to include the nearby village of Montescaglioso (in whose old town lesser kestrels also nest in large numbers). The flora is very rich and includes a thousand species, including real rarities such as *Stipa austroitalica, Campanula versicolor, Asyneuma limonifolium.*

As for fauna, many species of birds can be counted, beginning with the egyptian vulture, with one of the last pairs in southern Italy nesting here. Also noteworthy is the widespread presence of the roller along the gravina di Matera. Western whip snake, leopard snake (*Zamenis situla*), four-lined ratsnake, european asp and european pond turtle are common among reptiles surveyed, while the mammals include crested porcupines, badgers, foxes and martens.

The itinerary
In the centre of Matera it is impossible to count lesser kestrels: in fact, these raptors can be seen flying virtually everywhere! You can therefore follow the classic tourist itinerary that, between Sasso Caveoso and Sasso Barisano, passing through the squares and clambers up to the rock churches of Madonna di Idris, Santa Lucia alle Malve or Convicinio di Sant'Antonio. In the park area, experienced guides (the list is on the website of the protected area) lead visitors to the rock sites in a landscape of solitude and beauty carved into the sides of the *gravine*, tipical canyons of southern Italy, crossed by rivers dry for most of the year and attended by very interesting birds.

Internet
www.parcomurgia.it
www.parks.it/parco.chiese.rupestri.materano/Eindex.php

Giulio Ielardi

1. LANDSCAPES

Giulio Ielardi

Piedmont / Alpi Marittime Regional Park

PIANO DEL VALASCO

One of the most beautiful plateaus of the Alps, accessible only on foot though without difficulty, this is the heart of the largest regional park of Piedmont. Like its older brother the National Park of Gran Paradiso, the park of the Alpi Marittime owes its existence to the House of Savoy (the royal house of the Italian Kingdom, which lasted until 1946). When, a hundred and fifty years ago Vittorio Emanuele II visited the Valle Gesso, he was struck by the beautiful scenery and rich wildlife. Mayors of the area understood the benefits derived from royal presence and gave him exclusive rights to hunting and fishing. And so, two years later, the royal hunting reserve was born. The date of 1857 is still engraved on a wooden plaque on the top of the roof of the Bela Rosin chalet in the village of Terme di Valdieri. Much later came the park, which protects the area, and enhances it thanks to a network of trails of varying difficulty. Passable by almost everyone without difficulty is the trail that leads to one of the most beautiful plateaus, the Plain of Valasco.

Where
More than eighty lakes, the most southerly glaciers in the Alps, a flora that has around 2,600 species, chamois and ibex, 50 kilometers as the crow flies from sperm whales and fin whales that pass by on the Ligurian Sea: the attractions of the Alpi Marittime park are many and make it one of the most interesting natural areas in the Alps. Between Valletta and Rovina valleys, in the central part of the protected area, we find the highest peaks: Mount Argentera and Mount Gelasius, reaching 3297 and 3143 m respectively. Nearly 5,000 chamois, 700-800 ibex, most importantly marmots, also roe deer and wild boar (in the woodland) are among most frequently observed animals.

A few European mouflons come during the summer months from the nearby French national park of Mercantour. Seven pairs of golden eagle breed here: a very high density and a reliable indicator of the health of the ecosystem. Then there are the characteristic species of alpine and rocky areas like willow ptarmigan, black grouse, wallcreeper, chough. In addition, the park is in the forefront of a major Alpine reintroduction project of bearded vulture. Over a dozen specimens of this majestic vulture have already been released in the Maritime Alps. Consequently, sightings of their characteristic silhouette are becoming more frequent as one scans the skies. Of even more interest is the flora. The abundance of endemic and rare species is truly exceptional and listing only the most well known we have *Saxifraga florulenta*, *Potentilla valderia*, the Allioni cowslip. In all, as already mentioned, there are 2,600 species of which over 450 can be admired with no effort at all at the magnificent botanical garden of Valderia Alpine - one of the most beautiful in the Alps - named after the endemic *Viola valderia* that was first described precisely along the stretch of the bed of the river Gesso where the garden is now located (open from mid June to mid September).

The itinerary
Coming from the Po Plain, take the Turin-Savona highway as far as the Fossano exit; from here take SS road 231 to Cuneo, then SS road 20 to Borgo San Dalmazzo. Borgo San Dalmazzo is situated at the beginning of the three valleys where the four Park Municipalities lie: Vernante (Vermenagna valley), Valdieri and Entracque (Gesso valley), Aisone (Stura valley). Valdieri can be reached following the SP 20 up to the Gesso valley, turning off the SS 20 in Borgo San Dalmazzo (from Borgo to Valdieri 9km). From Terme di Valdieri village, follow the road that runs behind the spa building and over the stream - closed to motor traffic - and continue into the valley at the southern foot of Mount Matto. Along the long hairpins, which can be overcome with shortcuts, the road rises gradually through a forest of firs and larches. After crossing a last small ditch, after the last bend, you cross a rocky ridge and find yourselves overlooking the spectacular plateau. Here there is a spring, while on the left the river rushes from the *plateau* of Valasco in a series of waterfalls. In the plain the grassland is furrowed by the zigzagging of the river, whose banks rise in big boulders. At the bottom is an old turreted hunting lodge, recently restored (1.10 hours from Terme). The way back is the same as the way you came.

Internet
www.parcoalpimarittime.it

Trentino-Alto Adige / Provincial Park of Paneveggio-Pale di San Martino

VAL VENEGIA

Among the most beautiful and enjoyable of the Alps, the Val Venegia walking trip is a long but easy walk in the classic Dolomite scenery of pastures, forests and rocky cliffs of fairytale beauty. It takes about two and a half hours of gentle walking to make the 477m. ascent, along a comfortable cart track. We start from the park's Visitors' Centre, Paneveggio. From Venice, follow the A27 to Belluno, and then n.203 for Agordo, n.346 to Moena, finally n.48 to Predazzo. Located not far from Lake Forte Buso, along the main road n.50 that goes from Predazzo up to the Passo Rolle, the Paneveggio Visitors' Centre shows exibitions about the great forest of spruce, now known as the Forest of Violins for the resonant quality of its spruce, used by violin makers of the past. It tells also of the animals of the forest, most representative among which would certainly be capercallie and red deer. Not far away, a large enclosure allows you to observe a group of these large ungulates closely. From the Visitors' Centre is a shuttle bus to Pian dei Casoni, the starting point of the walk. There is also parking for cars and campervans at Pian dei Casoni, which charges a fee during the months of July and August (€ 3 for cars, € 6 for campervan, for the whole day).

Where
The park, situated in the eastern section of the Province of Trento, is characterised by three different types of landscape. The northern section is covered by the forest of Paneveggio, 2,700 hectares of spruce fir woodland which has been a protected area for a long time. The south-eastern section includes part of the Dolomitic chain of the Pale di San Martino. The western section is represented by a part of the porphyritic chain of the Lagorai.

There are many different natural environments: from rocky slopes and rubble areas to grasslands and Alpine pastures, from impetuous streams to calm stretches of water, from fir woods to mixed deciduous trees, from glaciers to peat bogs.

The itinerary
From Pian dei Casoni, you set off on foot along the wide cart track, almost level at first, leading to the valley. A little further on is the Venegia hut, with a second (fee paying) car park. Carry on parallel to the river Travignolo, where you can already admire the great rock face in the background which belongs to the Cima dei Bureloni, in the Cimon della Pala group. After a stretch of woods you find the Venegiota hut, at which both valley and trail turn south at the start of the Mulaz foothills. Further on, ignore the turning to the left that leads to the eponymous refuge, located at the Margherita fork at an altitude of 2571 m.

After the Piano del Campigol della Vezzana, strewn with large boulders, the climb begins - never hard - that leads to the saddle where you will find the hut Baita Segantini, 2170 m. This is our goal (2.30 hours after departure). From the hut, where you can refresh yourself with a hot meal, the vertical cliffs of the Cimon della Pala and Cima Vezzana look really very close at hand. In the fields around it's easy to hear the warning whistle of the marmots, standing in front of one of the entrances to their burrows. After this pause, you can opt to return along a different route. From the hut, descend towards the Passo Rolle and, once past the Cervino Hut, take the turning to the right to the Juribello hut, which stands in a clearing at an altitude of 1868 m. Now, following the arrows to the Pian dei Casoni, you enter the magnificent forest, descending rapidly to the valley and car park (1.30 hours from Baita Segantini).

Internet
www.parcopan.org

Trentino-Alto Adige / Adamello-Brenta Provincial Park

VAL DI GENOVA, HEART OF THE ALPS

At the heart of the Alps, the Adamello-Brenta park offers visitors one of the most beautiful landscapes of the mountain ridge. The so-called "waterfall trail" runs along the extraordinary Genova valley for its entire 15 km length, following the jewel of the park, the river Sarca. Wooden walkways that pass over the lateral tributaries make the journey easy and therefore suitable for everyone.

Where
The Adamello-Brenta park covers an area of 62,517 hectares and includes two completely different environments: the mountains of the Brenta Dolomites and part of the Adamello - Presanella massif. Fifty-one alpine lakes dot the protected area, starting with the Tovel lake made famous by the former reddish hue of its waters due to algae. Forests of beech, spruce, larch and pine cover about one-third of the park. Above the stretches of mountain pine begins the Arctic-alpine tundra, where the trees become sparse and one finds shrubs twisted from winter snow and an almost constant wind. *Loiseleuria procumbus*, White dryas (*Dryas octopetala*), *Linnea borealis*, are some of its endemic species of these precious habitats. Altitude forests and grasslands are also home to many of the stars of the fauna of the park from the red to the roe deer, from the chamois to the ibex (reintroduced after their disappearance in the second half of the seventeenth century due to indiscriminate hunting), from the marmot to the Alpine shrew. The bird count numbers a hundred species, including all five varieties of Mountain Grouse, the rare black woodpecker, numerous owls and a golden eagle population consisting of a large number of breeding pairs.

Thanks to a reintroduction project using specimens from neighboring Slovenia, dozens of brown bears now live in the park. And to the bear is also dedicated a beautiful wildlife area near the village of Spormaggiore, on the eastern edge of the park.

The itinerary
The trail itself begins in Ponte Verde, at an altitude of 900 meters, where there is a park information point. Ponte Verde is reached along the road between Pinzolo and Madonna di Campiglio, reached from Trento by the state roads 45bis, 237 and 239. From Ponte Verde start walking along the well marked trail. The first obligatory stop is in front of the scenic waterfalls of Nardis, which are just a few minutes into the walk. With gentle rises and falls the path then leads up to the Piani di Genova, a large grassy open space where you can make a short detour to the falls of the Lares,

which in three successive leaps reach over 200 meters. At nearby Ponte Rosso is another park information point. A stretch of the old paved road leads in half an hour to the typical Todesca and Ragada houses, with the little church of the Madonna di Ragada and the monument to the Pioneers of the Val Genova. Taking the path it's an easy climb to the grasslands of Casina Muta, beside lovely rapids and reaching the upper part of the valley. Near Caret plain and its eponymous hut, in a twenty minute walk, in the summer you can meet Rendena cattle with their unmistakable dark coat. Being careful, you can admire *Drosera* plants among patches of peat bog, a species that feeds on insects trapped in the sticky liquid secreted by glandular hairs that cover the leaves. Among scree and the occasional mound you reach the base of the Pedruc waterfall, which can also be seen from the top thanks to a daring wooden walkway. The trail then comes to an end in the plain of Bedole, after a drop of about 600 meters travelled in just over 4 hours. At an altitude of 1584 meters, the plain and its eponymous shelter are surrounded by the imposing amphitheatre of the Lobbie and Mandron glaciers. Here, the valley's shuttle service - a tourist service organized by the park - allows you to return in comfort or, if you still want to walk, you can retrace your steps to the Ponte Verde.

Internet
www.pnab.it

Friuli-Venezia Giulia / Regional reserves of Valle Canal Novo and Foci dello Stella

MARANO LAGOON

The most important Italian wetlands are to be found not far from Venice, along the low, sandy coast of the Northern Adriatic. One of these is the lagoon of Marano, an ancient fishing village, where "valli" (from the Latin *vallum*, bank) once used for fish farming today offer - with the adjacent reed marshes - an ideal haven to a wealth of wild birds.

Where
Together with the adjacent Grado lagoon, the Marano lagoon covers an area of 16,000 hectares between the mouth of the Tagliamento and the Isonzo, and is one of the largest Italian wetlands. The rivers of the lower Friuli plain guarantee an abundant inflow of fresh water, contributing to the enrichment of biodiversity. Part of the area is protected by two reserves. Valle Canal Novo reserve, a former fish farm, covers about 121 hectares near the town of Marano Lagunare. The management of the protected area is not only directed at the preservation of this fragile environment, but also to scientific research and environmental education.

The itinerary
To reach the nature reserve take the A4 Venice-Trieste motorway, exiting at Porpetto. Following the directions to the industrial area of Aussa-Como, after the town of San Giorgio, turn right and go to Carlino and then Marano Lagunare. To enter the reserve it is necessary to buy a ticket. The proceeds will be used to manage the reserve and reduce the financial burden on the part of regional and city autorithy. Cason Ristoro (casons are ancient typical fishermen buildings) has been converted into a

visitors' centre offering restaurant facilities, toilets and information. Inside it can seat groups of up to 60 people, who can enjoy their lunch in warmth and shelter or cool and shade, according to the season.

If you want you can also (by appointment) dine simply, enjoying some local dish; the *Casone* has a bar and kitchen. Here inside you can also request more information as well as purchase educational or informative materials. From the entrance of the reserve, having parked the car, you can visit the valley by walking along a wooden pier where, among the reeds, it is not difficult to see and photograph ducks, herons, and swans. You can also visit some other *Casoni*, typical fishermen's houses made of reeds, mud and wood, nowadays used as learning centers and places to eat. Adjacent to the valley is the other reserve of Foci dello Stella, 1377 acres, accessible only by punt (information and reservations at the visitor centre of the Valle Canal Novo reserve).

Internet
www.riservenaturali.maranolagunare.com

Liguria / Cinque Terre National Park

THE PATH OF LOVE

The Cinque Terre are among the most appreciated Tyrrhenian and Ligurian coasts, and not just in Italy. Fabulous villages hang over the sea on the edge of a rocky coastline softened by the geometry of the terraces. A giant staircase created by human hands, where the ancient terraces once cultivated with vineyards lie abandoned not only because of difficult access and the prohibitive cost of maintenance, but also as a result of social changes in the last century.

Where
Along this remarkable stretch of coastline the landscape is marked by (according to some calculations) almost two thousand kilometers of terraced bands - the result of traditional local agricultural organization dating from the early millennium. Monterosso, Vernazza, Corniglia, Manarola and Riomaggiore are certainly among the very few villages along the coasts of the entire Italian peninsula to have retained a genuine coastal stamp. The tortuous morphology of the territory, on the one hand, and a coastline full of cliffs, coves and small islands on the other, creates a landscape of great beauty which has inspired legions of artists beginning with the poet Eugenio Montale. Here, for centuries, generations of farmers have cultivated the vineyards clinging to the high cliffs dominated by ancient watchtowers that surround large creeks and wooded slopes, green with oaks, cork trees and Mediterranean scrub. At Cinque Terre there is also a marine reserve, protecting the waters and seabed, overlooking the park. It stands along a coastline of about 16 km, covering an area of 2,784 marine hectares, of which 100 enjoy full protection. The most beautiful reefs and rocky bottoms are at Punta Mesco and Capo Montenero, where there are outstanding biological

formations of great importance such as coral, twilight caves and coastal debris. There are also some small meadows and scattered patches of *Posidonia oceanica*.

The itinerary
We suggest the easy scenic trail n.2 of the park formerly named "Blue Path", linking Riomaggiore to Monterosso through the other three Terre named Manarola, Corniglia and Vernazza. The first portion of the path is actually known worldwide as "La Via dell'Amore" (the Path of Love), carved into the rock between 1926 and 1928 for connecting Riomaggiore to Manarola. Often interrupted by landslides and closed to pedestrian traffic, it has returned to its former glory after restoration work, however, it can never be considered safe. It is a pleasant stroll suitable for everyone. The base has been extended and embellished (there is also a "lovers' bench"). The railway stations of different villages are the step-points of this romantic road that winds along the top

of the cliff, making the train the ideal means of public transport to reach the starting point, and also for the return journey for those unwilling to do it again on foot. The estimated time of five hours is only indicative, because the ride is relatively easy and stops in the picturesque villages are a must. Among the significant points along the way we would mention the beach of Corniglia, the scenic village of Prevo (maximum altitude 208 m) between Corniglia and Vernazza, and the cultivations of olives, vines, lemons and vegetables of the basin dell'Acquapendente between Vernazza and Monterosso. It is worth underlining that, although on the sea front, the track is comparable to a mountain path: it is entirely appropriate, therefore, leave your beach shoes in the car and wear more comfortable shoes or hiking boots.

Internet
www.parks.it
www.parconazionale5terre.it

Emilia-Romagna / Tuscan-Emilian Apennine National Park

THE MOUNTAIN OF DANTE

Three hundred metres high, two hundred and forty wide and one kilometer long, the Bismantova Rock offers the most spectacular view of the Tuscan-Emilian Apennine National Park - one of the least known in Italy.

Where
The park protects one of the less frequented areas of the Northern Apennines, halfway between Tuscany and Emilia-Romagna. Thanks to the diverse habitats, the vastness of the territory and a limited human presence, its valleys and ridges are home to a rich and interesting fauna. Among the most significant presences for naturalists and visitors is that of the wolf, the adaptable predator returned to populate these mountains several years ago thanks to the abundance of ungulates. Roe deer and wild boar are numerous and widespread throughout the protected area, and it is not uncommon to see one or other on the edge of the forest, preferably in the twilight hours. More elusive and uncommon is the red deer, while it is possible to see small herds of wild sheep grazing in the summer on high-altitude meadows. In addition to larger species, the relatively intact environments of the park permit the presence of several other mammals such as marmots (introduced decades ago), badger, squirrel, marten and the polecat, fox, weasel, little dormouse and the rare (for the Apennines) snow vole - a true glacial relict. Bird life is well represented. Forest related species include various varieties of woodpecker, short-toed treecreeper, common crossbill, goshawk and sparrowhawk. Eagle owls, eagles and peregrine falcons can be seen, with a little luck and skill, in their rocky habitat, and the high grasslands provide the easiest observation points for numerous songbirds such pipit and linnet, alpine accentor and

black redstart. Along the streams the most representative species is the dipper, a sign of clean water, along with yellow wagtail and - among fishes - the brown trout, the roach, the barbel. European common frogs, newts, salamanders and italian cave salamanders are among the amphibians present. Also well represented are reptiles, with western whip snake, european asp, aesculapian snake, grass snake and slow-worm. From the walls of the Bismantova Rock, kestrel and jackdaws soar upwards in flight, while at night, lower down among fields and woods, roam wild boar and deer, hedgehogs and pheasants. The Triassic gypsum are among the oldest rocks of the Apennines, older than 200 million years, full of caves, sinkholes, crystals of all shapes and sizes. At Sorgenti di Poiano, along the banks of the river and in beautiful countryside, it is not difficult to surprise deer grazing, much less listen to the "laugh" of the green woodpecker.

There are many other sites of scenic interest, from Cascate del Lavacchiello to Calamone lakes, to Orecchiella. Here, on the Tuscan side, the Forestry Service in the three existing state reserves has already made several long trails, a visitor centre and some wildlife areas that are home to wild sheep, deer and brown bears. Among the numerous villages we report at least Castiglione di Garfagnana, Roccaferrara and the tiny village of Casenove near Ligonchio.

The itinerary
The Bismantova is a singular place, and has always been frequented by man. Dante Alighieri referred to it in his *Divine Comedy*: "Montasi su in Bismantova in cacume/con esso i piè; ma qui convien ch'om voli" (Purgatory, IV, vv.26-27). The massive calcarenitic block, 300 meters high, 240 wide and a kilometre long, sits on the Emilian side up to a thousand metres above sea level in a gentle landscape of fields, meadows and forest edges, and is undoubtedly the main attraction of the park. From Florence take the highway A11 "Firenze-Mare". From Lucca, take the road to Viareggio and reach the motorway Livorno Genova A12, go ahead towards Genova until the junction for Parma, and then take Autostrada della Cisa A15. Exit Aulla, then follow the road signs to Fivizzano and take SS 63 to Cerreto Pass. Head for Reggio Emilia. After crossing the pass, continuing along SS 63, you will find the junctions leading to Castelnovo ne' Monti. From Castelnovo ne' Monti you reach the square below in just a few kilometres, after which a trail leads to the summit occupied by meadows and woods, taking about an hour and a half to get there. From the top the view encompasses 360 degrees, taking in the nearby ridge at Mount Cimone, and extending to the Po Valley.

Internet
www.parks.it
www.parcoappennino.it

Emilia-Romagna / Foreste Casentinesi, Falterona, Campigna National Park

THE ACQUACHETA WATERFALL

This waterfall, one of the most beautiful in Italy, can only be reached on foot. An easy and comfortable path between cool woods reaches it along the banks of a stream. Acquacheta adds beauty to the fame it already enjoys from literature. It was none other than Dante Alighieri, in fact, who mentioned it in his *Divine Comedy* in order to compare it to Phlegethon, whose waters flow into the abyss in the eighth circle of Hell. The poet personally visited Acquacheta during a return trip from Florence to Forlì: it seems that he was deeply impressed, and no wonder.

Where
Twenty miles of ridge completely shrouded with leaves, trunks and branches embrace the heart of the most densely wooded national park in Italy. And under the green canopy there are the watery surprises: the Acquacheta waterfall, and then that of Scalandrini, the Oia stream, or the reservoir of Ridracoli itself. And how can we forget the monastery hermitage of Camaldoli, or the lush forest of Lama? The beauties of the Foreste Casentinesi, Falterona and Campigna national parks are too many to mention, though they certainly don't belong to an unknown or undiscovered Italy. Thanks to a network of facilities for tourism and hospitality with few comparisons among the Italian parks - from eleven visitor centers to nearly six hundred miles of trails - the beauty of this large protected area between Romagna and Tuscany is steadily becoming better known and appreciated. This is the Italian national park that, more than any other, covers a mainly wooded area: 31,222 hectares out of a total of 36,426 - more over 85%. Human history here has always

been intertwined with that of the natural environment. Let us remember that from these forests came the wood for the Florentine Opera del Duomo, or wood to build the powerful fleets of Pisa and Livorno. Here the Benedictine St. Romuald and his followers, at the dawn of the millennium, began to plant fir trees. And to this day Camaldoli with its centuries-old firs is one of the prettiest spots in the park. And here, finally, in 1959 the first wild nature reserve in Italy was founded - Sasso Fratino: a garden of Eden of great natural value, where only researchers can enter.

The itinerary
You can reach the park by taking the highway A14 (Bologna-Rimini), as far the exit of Forlì. From Forlì along Montone valley (SS.67), Rabbi valley (SS.9 ter) and Bidente valley (SS 310), you can reach Portico and San Benedetto in Alpe. We start walking from San Benedetto, from the car park along the river at the end

of the houses going up to the beautiful monastery of San Benedetto. The trail follows the river on the left side, going up easily through the sheltering forest of willows and alders. After several minutes you reach the small Molino Romiti, with one room used as a shelter in case of emergency. From here the route climbs the narrowing valley. After just over an hour, we find ourselves at the observation point of the waterfall, very scenic indeed. A total of about seventy feet high, the cascade is formed by the fall of water from the Acquacheta stream from the Piana dei Romiti in a sequence of steps and steep slides that expand and disperse the streams across a broad front of rock at least thirty-five metres wide. The substrate is of marl-sandstone formation, characteristic of this sector of the Apennines, and you can see the alternating layers of sandstone (hard and therefore resistant to the erosive force of water) and marl (easily eroded layers). From the observation point you can continue to walk along the path for a few tens of metres up to another waterfall: the "small one" of the Lavan stream. Then back the way you came to San Benedetto.

Internet
www.parcoforestecasentinesi.it

Tuscany / Bolgheri Natural Reserve

THE TREASURY OF MAREMMA

Between Cecina and the promontory of Piombino, beyond the Aurelia highway and the railway, is a piece of Italy's past. Here you can find all the typical environments of the Maremma, miraculously intact, in this order: the beach, the dune covered by Mediterranean scrub and pines, a large pond bordered by reeds, and cultivated fields bordered by hedgerows. In 1962 the first private wildlife refuge in the country was established, created by its owner Mario Incisa della Rocchetta, marquis and first president of WWF-Italy, to which the management of the reserve was immediately assigned after its inception in 1966. The State arrived later, in 1970, with the establishment of an oasis of protection from the Ministry of Agriculture. Today, as then, Bolgheri is still a paradise. The hectares of the farm number 2,700, those of the oasis 500. Surrounding the bog is a magnificent flooded forest, formed by narrow-leafed ash (*Fraxinus angustifolia*), elms, white poplars and tamarisks, that for a few months of the year find themselves with the roots immersed in water.

The itinerary
The oasis is open from April to November, with reservations required. For reservations and information please e-mail bolgheri@wwf.it or call 334 7584832. The visiting days are on Fridays, by appointment at 9 and at 14, and the first and third Saturday of each month at 9 and at 14. The meeting point is at the entrance plaza of the oasis, at km. 269.400 of the road Sp 39 "Old Aurelia." From Florence take the Firenze-Mare A11 motorway and then the junction south towards Cecina. From here, take the Via Aurelia towards Piombino, then the Vecchia Aurelia towards Bolgheri as far as the meeting point indicated.

From the observation tower near the entrance the view sweeps over the reeds and hydric wood, but it is by moving stealthily from one hide to another, along walkways well protected by a canopy, that one feels far away from everything and everyone, totally immersed in the wild world of the swamp. You can frequently see wild boar, foxes and deer, whereas the otter has sadly been extinct since the 1970's. The bird life is rich - according to the season, you can count on thousands of ducks and geese, cranes, herons, raptors and waders. Bolgheri is an important wintering place of a species becoming increasingly rare in Italy, the stock dove (*Columba oenas*). Among other rarities are the crested cuckoo, lesser spotted eagle, glossy ibis, and the lesser spotted woodpecker.

Internet
www.wwf.it/bolgheri.nt

Lazio / Circeo National Park

THE ISLAND OF SEAGULLS

Wild and uninhabited, not included in the Circeo national park until 1979, it is the only one of the Pontine islands to have preserved the integrity of its natural environment, demonstrating a blanket of lush Mediterranean vegetation. An hour of driving and another in a boat from Rome, Zannone is a hundred acres of wild Lazio, unique and unexpected.

Where
Established as early as 1934, the Circeo National Park is the oldest and most famous park in Lazio. Rich in habitat, despite its rather limited size, it includes the most beautiful beaches in the region, a rocky promontory, four coastal lakes, extensive and flat forest and the wildest of the Pontine islands. The largest environment is the state forest, a large green rectangle between the Pontina highway and the coast. This is what remains of the intricate Selva di Terracina, that before the great reclamation of the wetlands of Pontine extended over much of this coastal plain. Through the network of marked trails, the forest can be visited easily on foot or by bicycle. Palms and peregrine falcons live on the mountain of Circe, the legendary enchantress who according to Homer bewitched Ulysses and his companions on the journey back to Ithaca. Along the coast of the cape open the numerous caves. Birds are the greatest attraction of the four coastal lakes, all recognized as wetlands of international importance. Ponds full of fish, housing 45 different species include eels, sea bass, sea bream, sole and mullet. Not surprisingly, there is an abundance of fish-eating birds such as herons and cormorants, which are observed in the Circeo park easily alongisde black-winged stilt and flamingos, ducks and loons, hawks and more rarely (and in passing) osprey. Along the canals you can encounter turtles or

buffaloes from the many local farms that come to refresh themselves escorted by the inevitable cattle egrets. Then, off the coast, the wild island of Zannone also forms part of the park.

The itinerary
Zannone is a large volcanic rock, one thousand metres wide and fifteen hundred metres long, left without houses and without roads due to an unusual history of ownership, having passed from a Benedictine community to a rich marquis who loved to hunt, and then to the City of Ponza. Today in Zannone there are the ruins of the former caretaker's house, two lighthouses, the remains of a Benedictine monastery and a Roman fishpond - and nothing more. Daily guided tours, thus, carried out in the summer with a boat from Ponza island, offer the thrill of an almost untouched environment: aromatic stretch of gorses, phillyrea, mastic, and then the animals - beginning with wild

sheep (*Ovis musimon*), a few dozen having been introduced in the past for hunting, to the three breeding pairs of peregrine falcon, the one thousand nests of herring gull, and the greater shearwaters of the wailing night song. To get to Ponza - from where with tourist connections it is possible to visit Zannone island - you can use the shipping lines leaving from the ports of Formia (Caremar), Terracina (Mazzella), Anzio (Caremar), San Felice Circeo (Pontina Navigazione - note: seasonal line). From Rome head south along the Pontina highway. The island is a beauty. A cloak of lush Mediterranean vegetation covers it almost entirely, apart from around the old caretaker's house. From here, going up through the myrtle and heathers, you reach the summit of Mount Pellegrino, at 194 metres the highest point. The view extends over the island's hundred hectares, formed by eruptions of long ago - among the oldest of the territory which today we call Italian - which occurred until the Pliocene era, more than five million years ago. Via a detour you reach the lighthouse at Cape Negro on the north coast. From the lighthouse a concrete ramp allows you to get down to the rocks, and walking toward the west you come to a small beach, the only one on the island, made of pebbles and squeezed by the cliff that looms behind it.

Internet
www.parks.it
www.parcocirceo.it

Abruzzo / Gran Sasso and Monti della Laga National Park

THE ROOF OF THE APENNINE

The highest peak of the Apennines guarantees - clouds and mist permitting - the spectacle of a 360 degree view and a birds-eye view of all other peaks of the group and the other mountains of central Italy from the Tyrrhenian to the Adriatic, starting from Laga, Maiella and Sibillini. No particular technical difficulties reserve it only for mountaineers; the path from Campo Imperatore rises to a height of 2912m and can be covered by just about everyone. You need, however, a minimum of training and a pair of hiking boots or shoes, preferably already tested. The altitude difference of 800m is not considered excessive, given that it takes more than three hours to complete. Given the prolonged snow of the mountain, the hike is in any case carried out in summer or autumn, preferably starting early to enjoy a better visibility on arrival.

Where
The largest park of Abruzzo - third largest in Italy, after those of the Pollino and Cilento-Vallo di Diano - covers a huge territory stretching from the Apennine ridge to the valleys of the Tronto and Tavo. That is to say, from the three thousand meters of Corno Grande to the Pliocenic hills toward the Adriatic. It's a park with many faces, as is often the case in Italy. There are the solemn landscapes of the Dolomite peaks of Gran Sasso and the boundless horizon of Campo Imperatore, the world of lush forests and waterfalls of Laga, the ancient stone of the old towns, mighty castles, the Roman city and - even older - Italic settlements, the twilight of the secluded canyons and Gemelli mountains, exceptionally clear waters and an abundance of rivers such as the Tirino. And then the animals: most typical of the area is the chamois, who died out in these mountains at the end

of the nineteenth century. Just a century later in 1992, the first reintroduction in the Gran Sasso was among the pilot projects of the national park, with specimens taken from the nearby Park of Abruzzo, Lazio, Molise. The chamois is accompanied by golden eagles and peregrine falcons, wolves and bears, and then an endless list of species which illustrates more than words the health of ecosystems. The supreme biodiversity of the park enables it to count on well over 2400 species of flora, including precious endemics such as the edelweiss of the Apennines, the Mathilda's Rock Jasmine, the Spring Pheasant's (*Adonis vernalis*). Gran Sasso-Laga park is really second to none. Here - and nowhere else - are the highest peak of the Apennines, the largest plateau of the peninsula, the largest lake in Abruzzo, the southernmost glacier in Europe...

The itinerary
The spectacular plateau of Campo Imperatore is easily accessible from Rome along the highway A24 to L'Aquila and the subsequent exit of Assergi. From the car park end of the road that goes from Campo Imperatore, climb the trail to the left of the Astronomic Observatory, and with trail No. 3 (the first fork to the right) you will quickly reach the panoramic Sella di Monte Aquila, which dominates the valley of Campo Pericoli. From right to left, the amphitheater of peaks includes Corno Grande, Pizzo d'Intermesoli, Pizzo Cefalone, and Mount Portella. Towards the south, the horizon shows the massif of Majella. From Sella the path on the right, numbered 4 - the so-called "direct route" - rises up the rugged hillside south through the Sassone, and shortly reaches the top, though some passes require climbing at Grade II level. If you would rather not graps the rocks, instead, take the left trail no.3 that cuts halfway up the grassy slopes, past the junction for the Garibaldi refuge (20 minutes downhill) and then rises in hairpin bends to the Sella del Brecciaio, at an altitude of 2506 m. So far this takes about two hours from the car park. Following the trail No. 3 across the Conca degli Invalidi, you will find on your left the crossroads for Sella dei Due Corni, overlooking the Franchetti refuge. But if instead you turn right, there's nothing else but the exacting zigzag up the scree to the northern ridge, and from there you'll quickly reach the summit (1-1.5 hours from the Sella del Brecciaio). The descent along the same route takes a couple of hours.

Internet
www.gransassolagapark.it

Campania / Cilento and Vallo di Diano National Park

SECRET CAMPANIA

In 2011, this National Park has its twentieth birthday, but the Cilento is still truly a "world to discover." Gargantuan in size, with landscapes from mountains to coast, rich as only the Italian South could be.

Where
Between the Autostrada del Sole and the Tyrrhenian coast, the vast protected area (second largest in Italy after the Pollino national park) covers the entire face of the headland and the hinterland hills of the Cilento, up to the massifs of mounts Forcella, Gelbison, Cervati and Alburni. Natural resources are considerable and little known: beech woods and caves, cliffs and lonely rivers, two thousand botanical varieties including the

spectacular carob tree or the rare *Primula palinuri*, raptors and wolves, the most important peninsula populations of Apennine hare (*Lepus corsicanus*) and especially - otters. In the countryside, an agriculture that is still vital and diverse helps biodiversity and landscape variety. Along with the archaeological areas of Velia and Paestum and the Certosa di Padula (the latter two just outside the protected area), in 1998 the park was included in the prestigious Unesco World Heritage List. The northernmost area is occupied by the Alburni mountains. Made of white limestone of the Cretaceous era, these mountains are full of cavities such as the famous caves of Castelcivita (nearly five kilometers long) and those of Pertosa. In the heart of the massif rises the highest mountain, Mount Panormo or Alburno.

The itinerary
From Naples, follow the highway to Salerno, and from there continue towards Reggio Calabria. Continue until the exit of the A3 at Sicignano, where you exit following signs for Postiglione, then Castelcivita and finally Ottati. From Ottati, at the southern foot of the small but spectacular ridge of Alburni, we reach the Panormo refuge (1333 m), almost at the end of a paved road which starts at the end of the town and heads towards S. Angelo a Fasanella: a turning on the left with wooden signs. Leaving the car near the refuge, with restaurant and bar where you can take water for the trip, take the track going north-east, rejoining that which comes from Casone Farina after 15 minutes, on the ridge. After another quarter of an hour you get to the lower part of the well marked track "Sentiero Italia", (you will come to the higher part on the summit), which you follow round to the left through a beech forest. The red and white signs follow one another, but be careful not to lose sight of them - the geography of the place is really twisted, making orientation difficult. At the junction of Vuccolo Arena, altitude 1480 m (1526 m on maps), you can descend quickly on the left to a spectacular lookout on Sicignano,

that the Sentiero Italia reaches by a steep winding descent. From the Vuccolo, however, go right instead, up into the woods between the chasms of *grave* near which grow, thanks to the cool moisture, European yew trees (*Taxus baccata*). After forty-five minutes you will come out on a bare ridge, which you can climb among *Sempervivum* and thyme. At an altitude of 1742 m the peak is a panoramic balcony from Mount Pollino to the sea, from Mount Cervati to the other peaks of the park, to the Picentini mountains, to little towns perched on hilltops or embedded on the side of the valleys. Beyond the green mantle of beech forests of the Costa di Salvagnolo, which you will have just passed uphill, you can glimpse clearings near the refuge of Panormo, while looking along the east of the ridge, and walking for a while, you get to see the Figliolo rocky outcrop (1291 m), reached by an easy walk from Casone Aresta. From the start to the peak of Panormo, calculate two hours of walking. For the return you can follow the same route in about an hour and a half.

Internet
www.pncvd.it
www.parks.it

Sardinia / Gennargentu National Park

SUPRAMONTE COAST

Between Cala Gonone and Santa Maria Navarrese, west Sardinia, is the wildest stretch of Italian coastline. A continuous series of coves, pinnacles, heavenly beaches overlooking a sea that has few equals in the whole Mediterranean. It can only be seen from the water, thanks to the transportation service performed by various tourist boats.

Where
It would be one of the most extraordinary national parks in Italy and Europe, but it exists only on paper. Despite its formal establishment in 1998, the Gennargentu park in Sardinia has never been able to take off for a number of reasons, among which are the Sardinian claims for independence and the hostility of some municipalities. It includes the wildest inland environments of Sardinia, areas largely inhabited only by shepherds, flora and fauna of an exceptional interest, rugged landscapes, the most beautiful coasts of the Mediterranean. The contorted perimeter include at least four distinct areas. The first is the Gennargentu itself, with the Punta La Marmora (1,834 m) which is the highest peak of the island. To the north-east is the Supramonte, pure wilderness, calcareous environment and desolate stone horizons excavated by impressive canyons. Then there is the sea, which the park overlooks with an exceptional coastline: seen from the boat are the thirty-seven kilometers between S. Maria Navarrese and Cala Gonone - the longest stretch of wilderness in seven thousand miles of italian coast - a sight that takes your breath away. Finally, in the south, a strip of the park forms another unique landscape, the Ogliastra, characterized by rocky pinnacles of *tacchi* and *tonneri*.

The itinerary
Santa Maria Navarrese is reached from Cagliari by the n.125 road, after about 150 km. Leaving Santa Maria Navarrese the boat trip starts from the giant stack of Pedra Longa or Agugliastra, 128 meters high. Behind it follows a succession of rugged peaks such as Monte Argennas, the Punta Giradili, Monte Ginnircu. The sky above Capo di Monte Santu, a succession of high cliffs above which opens the wide crescent of the Gulf of Orosei, is host during the summer by slender silhouettes of groups of birds that weave their rapid trajectories - Eleonora's Falcon (*Falco eleonorae*), birds of prey that are very rare elsewhere, but here have one of the world strongholds, with dozens and dozens of breeding pairs. It is named in honor of Eleanor of Arborea, enlightened medieval Queen who first prescribed environmental standards for the protection of this unique bird of prey who divides his life between Sardinia in summer, and Madagascar in winter. After the Capo we meet the three inlets of portu Pedrosu,

port Quau (which means hidden harbour) and portu Iltiera. Shortly after comes the climax of the show: the indescribable turquoise waters in which the cala Goloritzé peaks are reflected. Continuing towards Cala Gonone, after other beaches and cliffs, we arrive at another well known place: cala Sisine. At the end of the eponymous *codula* (canyon) opens a jewel of a beach surrounded by rocks and the green forest of oak and juniper. After another five kilometres of vertical cliffs, caves and coastal forests we arrive at cala Luna. For those who see it for the first time, it's impossible to forget. The white beach stretches between the sea and a pond, bordered by oleanders and formed by the fresh waters of the river that runs through the *codula*. Six huge caves open further along on the north side, right on the beachfront in a natural setting of incomparable beauty. Three kilometres north of cala Luna the cliff is "bored" by another cave, the famous Bue Marino, which with its 4,200 meters of development is one of the main in the island. Its name and fame result from the presence, until a few decades ago, of the last Italian population of monk seal. Of the two branches of the cave, the north is equipped for tourism and has a complex series of tunnels and caverns flooded by the sea that goes inside the mountain. Ahead is the small bay of cala Fuili, already colonized by bathers, and then the touristy Cala Gonone. The boat trips usually depart from Santa Maria Navarrese, starting in the morning and returning in mid-afternoon.

Internet
www.parcogennargentu.it

Sardinia / La Maddalena Archipelago National Park

CALA COTICCIO

Cala Coticcio to Caprera is not only one of the wonders of the national park of La Maddalena Archipelago, but also one of the most extraordinary views of all the Italian coastal parks.

Where
Located in the northern part of Sardinia, it is probably the most beautiful marine national park in Italy. Islands and islets, mostly uninhabited, house colonies of seabirds that breed undisturbed. Successions of pink beaches and granite rocks create scenery to dream of, almost more tropical than Mediterranean. All around, a sea rich in life forms and extraordinary colors surrounds the edges of the earth. This is the real star of the Maddalena. Being the main island of the archipelago, La Maddalena is the only one to be inhabited. It has preserved a beautiful historic centre, and a winding road leads along the coast and inland to the meteorological observatory of Guardia Vecchia. Caprera, Garibaldi's island (Giuseppe Garibaldi is one of the chief figures of the Italian union), is the second largest but is second to none in the beauty of its beaches and coastline and its rich flora. Here there are pine and oak woods, evergreen patches of juniper and all the other Mediterranean trees, from myrtle to mastic, from strawberry tree to tree heather. Caprera is also home to a famous sailing centre in the Bay of Porto Palma. Then there are Spargi, Budelli, Razzoli and Santa Maria along the southern borders of the Strait of Bonifacio, microscopic worlds where the sea shows shades of colour not found along the rest of the Italian coast. At Spargi are the famous beaches of the east coast. As for Budelli, it's enough to mention the famous pink beach, immortalized in *Deserto Rosso* from director Michelangelo Antonioni, whose color is not due to the crumbling red rock as is sometimes erroneously

reported, but to the play of the currents that bring ashore tiny fragments of organisms such as foraminifera and bryozoans. At Razzoli you will be struck by the shapes of the rocks, whereas at Santa Maria by the beautiful beach. A myriad of small islands including Mortorio, Nibani and Soffi surround the islands, helping to make it a truly unique place in the Mediterranean.

The itinerary
To reach the starting point of the path, ie the Batterie Arbuticci, you need to reach Caprera from La Maddalena via the bridge of the Moneta and then continue for about two kilometers. After a detour to the left to Garibaldi's house, and another to Cala Brigantina on th right, there is a sign to a path marked with the number 2 and red and white signs. Do not miss a visit, either before or after the walk, to the fort of the so-called Batterie Arbuticci or Garibaldi, built along with many others on the island in 1887 as part of the fortifications that have periodically affected

the archipelago owing to its strategic position in the heart of Mediterranean. Having parked the car, you begin to walk among the granite boulders and lush patches of tree heather, strawberry trees and other evergreens, in air laden with aromatic essences. After initial ups and downs you pass a little military building and later begin to descend toward the sea, with glimpses of the Isolotti dei Monaci. This is the east coast of Caprera, and the only human tracks here are the boats that ply endlessly across one of the more celebrated seas in the Mediterranean. When you reach the isthmus of the promontory of Punta Coticcio, after a steep section of the trail that follows the path of some steps, you come first to a rocky bay on your left. However our goal is on the right, and appears as a white crescent set between the green shrubs and the incredible blue hues of the water. Walking between the rocks you can get to a second beach, slightly further on, bordered with junipers. The return is back the way you came and might take a couple of hours in all, including stops to rest.

Internet
www.lamaddalenapark.it

Giulio Ielardi

Sicily / Lampedusa Nature Reserve

THE TURTLE ISLAND

More Africa than Europe. Closer to Tunisia than Sicily. Lampedusa and its sea surround visitors with the vivid impressions of a distant, secluded land, the most remote corner of Italy lost in the sea of the Strait of Sicily.

Where
Italians go to Lampedusa for the sea. Beautiful, incredibly turquoise coloured. It stretches in front of an almost exclusively high and rocky coastline, which houses the nests of sea birds and hawks. The few beaches offer views of tropical white sand and the wild rocky kingdom of seagulls. In the restaurants of the village you can eat delicacies made with swordfish, amberjack or tuna. An African sun year-round warms residents and visitors,

the average temperature never below 15 degrees. These are ingredients critical to the success of many small tourist islands, but Lampedusa (and the smaller Linosa) have one more trump card, namely *Caretta caretta,* the sea turtle that for many years breeds on these beaches. In one night of early summer, the fertilized female comes out from the sea and goes to spawn (one hundred eggs, with diameter of a ping pong ball) in a hole laboriously dug with all four limbs. These eggs will take two months to hatch. This is the only kind of contact with the mainland for the turtle: exhausted from the egg-laying, the female covers the hole with sand and returns to the sea, like a robot driven by the evolution and instinct to live. Since 1995, a nature reserve protects 367 hectares of the most beautiful corner of the island, i.e. the famous beach of the Conigli (rabbits), which is where the turles have chosen to breed year after year. The protected area, which also includes adjacent stretches of coast, is managed by the Legambiente.

The itinerary
The island is reached by ferry from Porto Empedocle or with direct flights from Palermo, Trapani and - in summer - from Rome, Milan, Bologna. What do you do in Lampedusa, except of course sun bathing and sea? A good idea may be to rent a mountain bike or a scooter, preferably electric, and go to explore the island, more than eleven kilometers long and three wide. There is also a public transport service, which runs every hour through the island. The interior is almost devoid of vegetation, treeless except those planted by the Forestry and without settlements to attract visitors other than rare, authentic *dammusi* - low stone buildings - (imitations abound for residential tourism). If the north coast offers high cliffs full of caves, the southern and eastern instead have a number of sandy coves that are worth exploring. Apart from the road network, fairly wide between the east and the scenic point of Albero Sole - at 133 metres high the

highest point of the island - numerous dirt roads make easy terrain for bikes or horses (there's even a stable). Within the reserve are also several possible hikes to be carried out with guidance of Legambiente staff: the path from the Vallone dell'Acqua to that of Forbice, through reforestation of pine, acacia and carob, or the path to the beautiful Cala Pulcino. Or, again, the path of Cala Galera, between Mediterranean shrubs.

Internet
www.parks.it/riserva.isola.lampedusa/index.html

Sicily / Alcantara Regional Park

THE GORGE OF THE VOLCANO

At the foot of Etna a river has carved, over time, a bed of lava into astonishing forms. Its waters flow between black basalt cliffs, where canoeing is an exciting sport for (almost) everyone.

Where
Near famous Taormina, the Sicilian seaside is often crowded with tourists. The attractions of the greco-roman theatre, the sea, and Mount Etna looming over the landscape are irresistible magnets. Thus, it's up to the interior to offer the most unexpected sights. Pointing to the heart of the island towards Francavilla and Randazzo, between Castiglione and Gaggi, the world of the river Alcantara makes its appearance. A different horizon, a winding road through solitary landscapes instead of the busy coast road (not to mention the motorway A18 Catania-Messina), you'll find rows of rare oriental plane trees and willows instead of exotic palm trees and the ribbon of cars along the seaside. The Alcantara would be a river like any other, from mountain beech woods to the San Marco beach overlooking the Ionian Sea at Giardini Naxos, if Etna were not between the sea and the mountains. The largest active volcano in Europe is not only here to dominate the horizons, but with massive lava flows has, over the millennia, repeatedly interrupted and deflected the course of the river. The waters of the river must thus make their way among the banks of basalt, thereby giving rise to unique mineral landscapes, geotopes among the most outstanding of Italy and Europe. It's therefore a very special stream, protected since 2001 by a regional park. Dippers, freshwater crabs, brook trouts, yellow wagtails, stone curlews, and then green frogs and painted frogs (*Discoglossus pictus*) and the metallic blue coloured wings of the dragonfly: at Alcantara park they all still exist, thanks to integrity of

ecosystems and in particular a water quality that has elsewhere disappeared. The otter disappeared in the nineteenth century, here as in the rest of Sicily. On excursions along the river, it takes experience and luck to spot the presence of the several mammals such as hares and hedgehogs, martens, crested porcupines, garden dormhouse, maybe even the wild cat. Much more frequent are encounters with birds. The cliffs of the gorges are home to some very interesting species like the kingfisher and the blue rock thrush, in addition to the aforementioned yellow wagtail and dipper. The forests of the neighbouring countryside is home to - among other birds - sparrowhawks, hobbies, red kites, orioles and the local long-tailed tit (*Aegithalos caudatus siciliae*), while crops and grasslands are the habitat of quail and barn owl.

The itinerary
The most spectacular part of Alcantara valley, named Larderia Gorges, is in the territory of Motta Camastra. Access is by a staircase signposted along the road no. 18. Nearby, still along the road, an elevator access is available from a private company that also rents out, on request, the necessary equipment including wet suit, helmet, boots and life jacket. In fact, the only way to explore this part of the gorge is entering the water. The tour lasts an hour and a half. You go up the river for a long stretch without particular difficulty, between spectacular walls and then drift back down, carried by the current. Here the river erosion has revealed spectacular forms of lava - pipe-organs, harps, and fans. Length and difficulty vary, depending on the amount of water, its level and the relative velocity. In the gorges also you can meet animals such as frogs, rare snakes, swallows.

Internet
www.parcoalcantara.it

Giulio Ielardi

3. PLANTS

Giulio Ielardi

Lombardia / Palude Brabbia Nature Reserve

THE SECRET MARSH

The Palude (marsh) Brabbia is an expanse of reed, marshes and forests south of Lake Varese, derived from a peat bog that during the mid-19th century had been intensively exploited for the extraction of peat. Today it is one of the most interesting places for bird watching in crowded Lombardia.

Where
Protected since 1983 by a nature reserve established by the Lombardia Region and managed by Province of Varese and Lipu (Italian League for Bird Protection), the Palude Brabbia is an artificial environment. Here, in fact, the old peat "quarries", now unused and flooded, have become shallow ponds, surrounded by thickets of willow and alder and often covered by duckweed. The

protected area covers 459 hectares and is recognized as a wetland of international importance under the Ramsar Convention. In summer white water lilies bloom in the ponds with *Nuphar luteum*, but the marsh lily that blooms a few months before will have withered by then. Also to be found is a small carnivorous plant, the *Drosera*, which catches insects that carelessly find themselves on its glue trap. One hundred and forty species of birds have been recorded in these special surroundings, including nine species of duck and a dozen birds of prey. Also present is a small breeding population of the rare ferruginous duck and over a hundred breeding pairs of night, grey and red herons. The symbol of the oasis is the water rail, an elusive *rallidae* with long red beak that can sometimes be admired for a few moments when it comes out from the reeds to feed.

The itinerary
To reach the reserve you drive along the A8 motorway Milan-Varese to Buguggiate/Azzate, following the signs for Bodio Lomnago and then Inarzo. Here follow the main road for a kilometre to a large car park on the right, opposite the visitor centre of the reserve and Lipu oasis. Entrance is free every day from dawn to dusk. Along the paths are different hides with slits to see, and not be seen by, the birds that frequent the ponds. A classroom used as a small museum is used as support during the guided tours and lectures for school groups. From March to October, the Lipu also organizes excursions on a boat on nearby Lake Varese on Sundays: in two hours of sailing an expert explains the flora, fauna, curiosities and problems of the lake (you need to book in advance by phoning tel. 0332 964 028 or by writing to oasi.brabbia @ lipu.it).

Internet
www.lipu.varese.it

Veneto / Dolomiti Bellunesi National Park

BUSA DELLE VETTE

Established in 1990, the Dolomiti bellunesi national park is the only one that protects one of the most famous Italian landscapes in the world: namely that of the Dolomites. In addition to the landscape, the greatest natural resource is the flora. In fact, botanists have conducted numerous studies documenting the wealth of rare species, which motivated the proposed establishment of a national park. One of the sites most rich in flora is the Busa of the Vette, a basin reached on foot by a difficult path over a thousand metres in altitude. But it's worth it.

Where
The national park is mostly a wilderness of high mountains, where the boundaries are for the most part at high altitude and the settlements are concentrated in a narrow band around the edge. One hundred thousand inhabitants are registered here, but only 88 actually live inside the boundaries of the protected area, according to the last census. Among the major mountain ranges, whose peaks often exceed two thousand metres, are the Alpi Feltrine, Monti del Sole, Schiara-Pelf and Talvena. People come here to walk through magnificent scenery, along the valleys, admiring plants that already attracted the botanists of the eighteenth century, to see the eagles fly against a background of glacial cirques and vast pine forests.

The itinerary
We start from Passo Croce d'Aune, which is easily reached from Feltre - where the offices of the park are situated – by road n.473 toward Fiera di Primiero-San Martino di Castrozza. Feltre is located thirty kilometers west of Belluno, a town easily reachable from Venice by the A27 motorway. At the Passo Croce d'Aune,

at an altitude of 1011 m, you park near a kiosk that houses an information point belonging to the protected area, and start to walk following the white-red signs. The path coincides with a stretch of the Alta Via delle Dolomiti No.2 and therefore shares the signs. The first section is the most uncomfortable, because of rocks and mud that make it difficult to walk in the woods (beech giving way to spruce). It should be better when you get out in the open, after passing the last alders, where there is a military road that rises in one hairpin bend after another (trail 801). Created in 1918, the road encircles the south slopes of Pavione, Col di Luna and Vette Grandi. In some places the military road is cut into the rock and on this partition wall can be observed, from May onwards, interesting blooms of *Primula auricula, Pinguicula* sp., *Rhodothamnus chamaecistus* and the uncommon *Saxifraga burserana*. By taking both the road and steep shortcuts, we arrive at the Dal Piaz hut after two and a half hours.

We are almost at our goal but no one would think it. In fact we only have to walk a few minutes from the shelter to find ourselves suddenly on the panoramic balcony of the Passo Le Vette Grandi (1999 m). From here opens a view of the Busa delle Vette, one of the most spectacular suspended glacial cirques, minutely carved by karst. What is most striking are the wide open spaces of Busa, that take one completely by surprise in the middle of this ridge of sharp peaks. Two, two and a half kilometers of pastures which in early summer (and certainly from June to August) provide a sample of the exceptional flora which the park was set up to protect. One of the rarest is *Alyssum ovirense*, a pre-glacial species that in July tinges the screes with yellow. The southern part of the Busa, the one closest to Passo Le Vette Grandi, is riddled with small, densely packed sinkholes, while at its north it merges with the white spots on the margins of alluvial fans that descend from Vette Piccole, Cima Dodici, Costa dei Piadoch. All around the valley, half way up, a particular red geological formation called Rosso Ammonitico colours the short cliffs. What a show! In the bottom of the Busa, clearly visible, are the La Faora canyon and Vette Grandi hut, easily reached along a road, and where in summer you can taste the cheeses of the park. The return is back the way you came and takes about two hours.

Internet
www.dolomitipark.it

Emilia-Romagna / Po Delta Regional Park

PUNTE ALBERETE FLOODED FOREST

The Po Delta is defined as the Italy's most important wetland, and also one of most relevant in Europe. This is due to the unique landscapes, the incredible extent of reed beds and valleys of water, and the abundance of wildlife and biodiversity.

Where
The natural park of the Po Delta was set up in 1988 by the region of Emilia-Romagna for the protection of this extroardinary paradise. It protects stunning wetlands, the last stretches of plane forest, sandbanks and salt marshes. All the historic features of the landscape, i.e. land occupied until the last centuries by the river delta, line up along the coast south of the Po di Goro, the northern boundary of the park. After endless hydraulic works and massive land reclamation, the present delta has, so to speak, migrated north, leaving behind it many watery traces of its presence. In many cases, however, it is in these environmental "ruins" that an incredible abundace of natural richness is concentrated, rather than in the Delta itself. And the various sectors that comprise the protected area are like natural oases in a highly man-made territory. In these sixty thousand hectares of land, patchy but rich in nature values, landscape, history and art live side by side with the mosaics of Ravenna and straight flights of large flocks of ducks, rather than Trepponti of Comacchio and the expanse of flowering waterlilies in Campotto. Here, every visit is a great show and the Delta Park never disappoints.

The itinerary
Punte Alberete is 10 km north of Ravenna, which is reached with by state road n.309 Romea, about 80 km south of Venice. You can park your car in the car park along the Romea, at the

entrance of the forest, or on the opposite side of the road near the Visitor Centre Ca' Vecchia of June 2nd Park in the pine forest of San Vitale. In any case it is very important not to leave valuables in the car parks, because they have long been targeted by thieves. We enter the woods. We are in one of the most precious sites in the park of the Delta, a relic of a past when large portions of land and lowland plane forests were flooded by the freshwater outflows, now mostly channeled into the Lamone river. The trail is easy to spot and easily passable. After crossing a small pedestrian bridge over the Fossatone channel, we arrive in a green forest of willows, ash, poplars, elms, oaks, with intricate lianas of wild clematis and ivy. Large expanses of water open here and there, where magnificent flowering water lilies and *Salvinia* form a green carpet floating on the water. These pools are home to interesting small vertebrates, such as the marsh turtle, fishes of different varieties, newts, frogs and molluscs.

Here and there, in spring, you will see the showy deep yellow flowers of the lily swamp. The route is circular (it needs at least a couple of hours) and leads to some observation huts, well positioned for the sighting of numerous species of birds including the night heron, water rail, and ducks like rare ferruginous duck and red-crested pochard. For grey and red herons, nesting in Punte Alberete, but
also for spoonbills, squacco herons, ibis and pygmy cormorant, however, the best place is the large, high watchtower of Valle Mandriole, soon north along Romea road.

Internet
www.parcodeltapo.it

Marche-Umbria / National Park of Monti Sibillini

THE RING OF THE VALLEY OF PILATO

What is now protecting the majestic Sibillini chain is one of the most beautiful national parks emerged in the Nineties. For twenty miles, towering mountains line up to form a wall of limestone which at its southernmost point rises in regional watersheds.

Where
These are the majestic Apennines, strongly competing with the best-known Abruzzo section, including several "two thousand-ers" such as Monte Rotondo (2102 m), Mount Priora (2332 m), Bove (2,112 m), Porche (2173 m) , Argentella (2200 m), Carrier (2476 m). No wonder the snow remains for several months a year, and summer is the best season to discover its beauty from valley to peaks - and for making the trip that we describe. In ancient times glaciers stretched along here, and today there are plenty of traces including cirques, deep, typical "U" shaped valleys, or indeed the characteristic little lake of Pilato, one of whose most celebrated guests is the famous Chirocefalo of Marchesoni. It's also the most rare, since this tiny crustacean (only a few mm. long) does not live anywhere else. Chirocefalo aside, the fauna of the park includes many others such as wolves, wild cats, roe deer, golden eagles, peregrine falcons, hawks and owls, rock partridges, Orsini's snakes. Another great treasure of the park is the flora. Almost two thousand species live here and their popular show is repeated every year, usually in early June. The vast expanse of the plains of Castelluccio, main attraction of the park, is covered in a patchwork of colours, millions of flowering lilies, poppies, daisies, and also the famous lentils, of which a particular mountain variety is cultivated here.

The itinerary
To reach the park you come from north or south-east along the A16 Adriatica highway to the tolls of Macerata, Pedaso or San Benedetto del Tronto; from the south you can access the area on its west side, following the A1 to Orte, then the road along Nera Valley (Valnerina), or from east on the A1 up to Fiano Romano and then on the state road n.4 Salaria, touching Rieti and Antrodoco. When you arrive in Norcia, follow the signs for Castelluccio. The start of our journey on foot is from the Capanna Ghezzi (1570 m; where there is a fountain to fill water bottles), reached by a track from the plains of Castelluccio (the last right turn before the climb to the village, coming from Norcia). The path climbs with several bends up grassy knolls to Forca Viola (1936 m), taking about an hour. From here going to the right it winds up the side of the mountains surrounding the valley of Lake of Pilato, gaining altitude with wonderful views of the underlying Castelluccio plains, among blooms of yellow and

Dinaric gentian and *Dryas octopetala*. After Cima dell'Osservatorio (2350 m) you reach the ridge (here white/red signs disappear) overlooking the valley of the lake. Cima del Redentore (2448 m) and Cima del Lago (2422 m) are reached by continuing along the ridge, the most beautiful section of the trip. From subsequent Punta di Prato Pulito you descend without a path to Sella delle Ciaule (2240 m), following a rocky, treacherous ridge on which you must walk carefully. On the saddle is the small Zilioli shelter, built in masonry, with a room that is always accessible, furnished with simple bed-tables for two to three people and another room with key (to be taken in Forca di Presta). So far the journey is approximately 4 hours, making a few stops. On the horizon appears the Gran Sasso, while at night the towns of the Tronto valley resemble an illuminated nativity glowing in the dark. From the hut, surrounded by meadows full of Apennine edelweiss (*Leontopodium nivale*), you can gain the summit of Mount Vettore in an hour there and back. Continuing down the ring on the grassy slope toward the lake, you can once again, between the rocks, find the path marked in red. Finally the lake appears, with Cima del Redentore behind, half an hour from the hut. Abundant blooms of bluebells and, on the screes, of *Asperula neglecta* (with yellow flowers). In the waters of the lake (1940 m) it is easy to see the Chirocefalo of Marchesoni, the rare, tiny, bright red crustacean. It's worth mentioning that swimming is prohibited, as is getting close to the banks, in order not to crush the eggs of the crustacean. Immediately downstream from the mirror-like surface of the lake (at low water it splits into two) is the Fount of the Lake, where you can drink. From here, while the main path leads down to Foce, turn instead to the left along tracks that, without losing altitude, cross the screes leading to Forca Viola. Here are many beautiful *Drypis spinosa*, with white flowers and a myriad of soft thorns. You then decisively go up, between rocks and flowers of all kinds, to windswept Forca Viola. Here you begin the descent back the way you came to Capanna Ghezzi, taking altogether four hours' walk from Zilioli.

Internet
www.parks.it

Abruzzo / Majella National Park

THE FOREST OF SANT'ANTONIO

Second in height after the Gran Sasso along the ridge of the peninsula, the Majella is a mighty plateau of rock that has more than sixty peaks two thousand metres high, including Mount Amaro, reaching a maximum altitude of 2793 meters. Thick forest and wild valleys, especially on the eastern side, form the crown of the plateau, real deserts of stone on top of the mountain, where we find the harshest trails in the park. The forest of Sant'Antonio is perhaps the most beautiful, not far from Pescocostanzo, where huge beech trees as much as six centuries old spread out spectacular gnarled and twisted branches.

Where
The park is vast and covers approximately 74,000 hectares in south-central Abruzzo. The beech forest is in general the most common environment of the park, beyond which, at 1700 meters high, we find wonderful expanses of mountain pine (*Pinus mugo*). At lower altitudes are mixed forests of oak, turkey oak, hornbeam and flowering ash. The national park is home to 1,800 species of flowers, of which about one-tenth are endemic. As for the latter, they range from *Ranunculus crenatus* to *Viola magellensis*, from *Aquilegia magellensis* to *Androsace mathildae*, from *Adonide distorta* to *Centaurea tenoreniana*. During the summer the high grasslands are punctuated by blooms of *Gentiana dinarica* and *lutea*, *Lilium martagon*, the silene and the precious *Leontopodium nivale*, only present in the rest of the Apennine ridge on the Sibillini and Gran Sasso. Among the animals is the wolf and the bear, as well as the wild cat and the increasingly rare otter, chasing barbel and brown trout in the clear waters of the rivers Orta, Orfento and Vella. A Caramanico Terme, an animal park allows the observation of some specimens, especially during the first and last hours of the

day. Other important appearances in the park are the result of wildlife management operations. We are talking about red deer, roe deer and chamois, extinct during the last century and now again roaming free up the mountain. The first to return were red and roe deer, to the great benefit of the health of the local wolf population. From the early nineties the Abruzzo chamois arrived, having been extinct for some time. In the wetter gorges on the bottom of the valleys you may encounter some species of amphibian, including the yellow-bellied toad and the spectacled salamander. Among the reptiles, the Ursini's viper is one of the most significant, while among insects, with thousands of species present (Rhopalocera, ie butterflies, amount to a good 116), one of the most beautiful is certainly *Rosalia alpina*. Finally, among the birds, it's enough to mention only some of the most illustrious guests such as the golden eagle, lanner falcon, the goshawk, white-backed woodpecker and the wallcreeper. But the real surprise of the heart of the park is something else, and we find it higher up, in that stony landscape which is the priveleged environment of the park. We are talking about dotterel, a small wading bird that represents the most unique species in the Majella. Trapped in this part of the Appenines by the retreat of the Quaternary glaciers, thousands of kilometres from its environment of choice, up here it lives in a stone desert swept by snow and wind.

The itinerary
The forest of San Antonio lies in the municipality of Pescocostanzo at the southern end of the park. To get here you take the motorway A25 from Rome to Pescara and exit at Sulmona. About 30 km from here along state road n.17 you reach Roccaraso and after a short detour you get to Pescocostanzo. To reach the forest, which covers the Colle della Difesa in an expanse of approximately 70 hectares, you should follow the signs to Cansano and Campo di Giove. The visit to the forest

does not provide a precise route, because there is no real path through it. You can park your car at the School of Cross Country Skiing, along a road about 1300 meters above sea level, and enter the beech forest to the right of the road. Moving freely or along the many tracks created by grazing cows you walk among beech trees, sometimes of a really solemn size. It is not difficult to see many of the inhabitants of the forest, such as the woodpeckers (present here is also the rare lesser spotted woodpecker and dalmatian woodpecker), wild boar, roe deer and red deer. It takes a little luck, however, to admire in spring the flowers of wild peony and the rare orchid *Epipactis purpurata*: throughout Abruzzo they only live here.

Internet
www.parks.it

Puglia / Gargano National Park

MONTE SACRO

This expanse of 118,144 hectares is located in the area of 19 municipalities all in the Foggia district. It's the Gargano National Park, one of the most beautiful in the south of Italy. It includes very different natural environments, from coastal cliffs to the Foresta Umbra, from wetlands to sinkholes, from dunes to limestone valleys. Its botanical value is very high.

Where
Over two thousand species of flowers form the more elegant of the extraordinary plant wealth of the park. Many are endemic species - including *Campanula garganica*, *Cystus clusii*, *Inula candida* - and of particular importance is the abundance of orchids (56 + 5 sub-species), one of the greatest number of varieties to be found in the entire European continent. As for wildlife, among mammals the most valuable species is the rare Italic roe deer. In forest environments you can also encounter wild boar, squirrels, garden dormouse, feral cats and, among birds, woodpeckers, buzzards, and sparrow hawks. Steppe areas at the foot of the promontory host perhaps the last bustards of the Italian peninsula and also stone curlews, calandra lark and lanner. In the large wetlands is an abundance of species, including flamingos and spoonbills, herons and black-winged stilts, ospreys and storks. Rocky coastal environments, finally, offer shelter to species like the peregrine falcon, pigeon, and Alpine Swift.

The itinerary
The walk is recommended for everyone, covering just over half an hour in a vertical drop of 250 meters, allowing you to get closer - in spring – to one of the richest areas in botanical terms of the protected area. The Gargano is reached by motorway A14

Bologna-Taranto, exit at Foggia. From here follow the main road n.89 to the coast towards Mattinata. About four kilometres beyond the town, at km 142, on the left climbs a steep detour road. Shortly after, the deep incision of valle della Vecchia appears on the right, one of the most interesting areas of the park, especially in the spring when many species of orchid are in flower. Ignore several junctions, the last of which on the left leads to a farm, and after a few km a park sign at Stinco signals the beginning of the path. Monte Sacro is a wooded hill that rises on the right-hand side of the road. Walk along the south-east side, starting in an open environment, and then into a copse of oaks, following the occasional red marks on the rocks.

In half an hour you reach the solemn ruins of Ss.Trinità abbey, built in medieval times on a temple to Jupiter Dodoneo. Abandoned by the Benedictine monks in the fifteenth century, it retains among the vegetation majestic traces of arches and

portals, capitals, a bell tower, fragments of frescoes. Beside a green plateau lie the remains of an older nucleus, which includes a series of pointed arches. Carefully exploring the small plateau of karst sinkholes cloaked in ferns, here and there you can glimpse views of the Mattinata valley, Mount Spigno, and the sea. In addition to the
black goats of Gargano, you can frequently see ravens and lanner falcon. You return the same way you came.

Internet
www.parcogargano.it

Basilicata / Pollino National Park

THE PINES OF THE "GRANDE PORTA"

Among the most beautiful walking routes in the Italian parks, this leads to the heart of the Pollino Massif – in Basilicata but on the border with Calabria - a dive into the unspoiled natural habitats of Southern Italy. With its almost two hundred thousand hectares, this national park is Italy's largest.

Where
The rocky slopes are its best feature. Its twisted and solemn shape stands on the highest peaks of the massif. Of the approximately ninety species of pine trees that grow in the world, bosnian pine (*Pino leucodermis*) is certainly among the most rare and endangered. Of pioneering character, able to settle even in an adverse environment, it owes its Italian name (*pino loricato*) to the large polygonal scales of bark, similar to the *lorica*, the metal plates of the ancient Roman armour. Damaged by fires and felling everywhere, now only a few grow in other regions of the southern Apennines. The area where it is more widespread, however, is the Balkan Peninsula, where botanists believe the species arrived during the glacial period. A few thousand have survived in the park of Pollino, in particular on the Serra di Crispo, Serra delle Ciavole and Serra Dolcedorme. Bosnian pine is the symbol of the national park.

The itinerary
From Naples, the Pollino Park can be reached via the highway to Salerno and then the A20 towards Reggio Calabria. From the Campo Tenese toll, climb the mountain towards San Severino Lucano, to the Colle dell'Impiso. There is a crossing at an altitude of 1573 meters, just ahead of the Piano Ruggio where you will find the De Gasperi hut. Leave the car on the side of the road,

cross over a bar and follow a short dirt road that climbs into the forest, then descend in the direction of the first of the small Piani di Vacquarro. Walk up to the junction with the trail that, to the right, would lead via Colle Gaudolino to the summit of Mount Pollino: we go left instead. Re-entering the forest, we reach the crystal clear waters of a stream where wading is easier, before tackling the long climb through the beech. Ignoring the turnings we emerge at the edge of the spectacular Piani di Pollino after about an hour and a half climbing, the more difficult part in the final stretch. On the left there is the view of the Serra di Crispo with its magnificent bosnian pines, on the right Mount Pollino and behind Serra Dolcedorme.

Go left into the meadows, climbing in the direction of some small isolated beech trees that indicate the precious Toscano spring (just behind the trees in a hollow of the ground). In May and June, having thawed recently, the slopes are riddled with holes:

these are the entrance to the voles tunnels. The meadows are carpeted with violets, *Scilla*, orchids and *Crocus* by the thousand. In another half hour, at the edge of a rocky cliff, you can reach the first pines, the elegant conifer which is the symbol of the national park. A little further on there is what remains of the great pine of the Grande Porta (great gate) del Pollino - the name assigned to the saddle between the Serra delle Ciavole and Serra di Crispo. This pine is reproduced in the logo of the protected area. The most majestic tree of all, it was adopted as a symbol of possible social change and consequently set on fire by vandals in the autumn of 1993, just after the establishment of the park. It is centuries old. Fortunately, other giants remain, such as on the Serretta della Porticella, the smaller peak on the ridge that you meet going up to the Serra di Crispo from the Grande Porta. These trees are still healthy, judging by the gray bark in large polygonal flakes, ranked alongside dead specimens still standing. Silver trunk and branches, often split by lightning, two thousand metres above sea level, defy wind and snow and cling to the back of limestone suspended on the mantle of Fagosa green below. As far as the Grande Porta, the difference in altitude is 374 metres and takes about three hours to climb. Without prolonging the excusion, which you could continue at will, descend from here to the Piani di Pollino and from there to the Colle dell'Impiso (allow an hour and a half from the Toscano spring).

Internet
www.parks.it
www.parcopollino.it

Calabria / Sila National Park

IN THE GIANTS' SHADOW

Not everyone knows, this but the south of Italy, land of sun and sea, cliffs and scorched fields of garrigue, also has its own corner of Scandinavia. It's the Sila, included in one of the lesser known Italian national parks. In summer it is a refreshing oasis with its unlimited "northern" pine woods and in winter it is often left alone, buried under metres of snow.

Where
Sila is a plateau between 1,100 and 1,700 meters in altitude, consisting of a large granitic-crystalline massif. The highest peak is Mount Botte Donato, 1929 m. The massif slopes to the south and east to the Ionian Sea, while to the north it borders the plain of Sybaris, and to the west the valley of the Crati river that separates it from the coastal Apennine mountain. The entire area is covered by forests, broken in Sila Grande only by the pastures of Macchialonga and Santa Barbara - or by lakes, all artificial, created in the 1950's for the production of electricity (except Vutturino, used for irrigation). Very similar to the Sila Grande and located further south, beyond the lake Ampollino, is Sila Piccola, the area of the park that preserves perhaps the most uncontaminated and beautiful corners. Here lies the wilderness that so enchanted Norman Douglas, who described it in his *Old Calabria* published in 1915. Even today, the environment more represented in the national park is the forest, rich in varieties such as beech and fir, but dominated by the typical local pine *Pinus laricio*, also present in Sicily, Corsica and Tuscany - which sometimes reaches venerable age and great size. In the higher areas the pine joins the beech, while in the lower we find turkey oak, chestnut and sometimes downy and sessile oak. At the bottom of the deeper valleys, where it's moist and shady, the

pines give way to Italian alder (*Alnus cordata*), aspen and rare white spruces. In thick pine forests undergrowth is generally poor, due to the dense shadow and accumulation of layers of needles on the ground. Among the few plants that are found there is common bracken, once used by Sila shepherds to make *ricotta* and *mozzarella*. In the clearings and at the edges of the forest grow shrubs such as goat willow (roe deer like it in winter), hawthorn, wild rose, holly, wild apple and pear trees, and broom. Violets, crocuses, daffodils and lilies are among the most showy flowers, which are accompanied in spring by several species of orchids such as *Orchis sambucina, O. papilionacea, O. laxiflora*.

The ubiquitous fungus, which in autumn attract large groups of mushroom-lovers, from the Saffron milk cap (*Lactarius deliciosus*) to the famous Porcino (*Boletus edulis*), from *Boletus luteus* to Parasol mushroom (*Macrolepiota procera*), from *Morchella* sp. to *Amanita caesarea*, the forests of the park will offer a very rich and varied collection. As for the fauna, the wolf is certainly the most representative animal of the park. On summer nights, at Fossiata wood, it isn't difficult to hear the repeated howls of some specimens moving through the forest. To encourage their numbers, the park has long been involved in a program of reintroduction for roe and red deer. Up in the trees, or for fleeting appearances on the ground, one more frequently encounters squirrels, the southern varieties characterized by black livery. In addition, wild boar, foxes and hedgehogs and, among birds, almost all woodland species - including the goshawk - are among the most conspicuous animals that you may encounter in any season.

The itinerary
Among the pine forests of the park, one of the largest and most fascinating is that of Fossiata, not far from Camigliatello. In the area of Fallistro are the most impressive specimens, the so-called giants of Sila. To reach it you go from Naples towards Reggio Calabria on motorway A3 and exit at Cosenza. Here you follow the road No.107, which quickly climbs to the plateau of the Sila. After Camigliatello Silano, continuing in the direction of San Giovanni in Fiore, we arrive at the area of Croce di Magara where there are signs by the Corpo Forestale (Forestry commission). Having parked the car, you enter on foot along an easy and quick circular path in the spectacular Bosco Fallistro, made from fifty-three pine trees, along with five Sycamore (*Acer pseudoplatanus*) trees, older than about four hundred and fifty years. The largest pine tree has a diameter of six feet and stands about 45m high. Colossal pines are also found in the area of Gallopane and into the Gariglione woods, where enormous firs and beeches also grow. Notably, the fir trees of Sila have shown particular resistance to acid rain, which is why their seeds have been requested in countries like Austria and Germany.

Internet
www.parcosila.it

Sicily / Etna Regional Park

BIRCHES ON THE VOLCANO

At 3340 metres, this is the highest active volcano in Europe. We're talking about Mount Etna, star of Sicily's outstanding countryside, an open-air laboratory where the landscape constantly changes and trekkers walk between ancient and recent lava flows, caves - there are over two hundred - and forests of larch, pine and beech. And birch. In fact, the protected area is home to one of the most valuable endemic plants of the island.

Where
Despite the presence of paved roads, ski resorts, deforestation and poaching, the Etna park houses significant wildlife. Among the species there are porcupines and wild cats, martens, rabbits, hare, garden dormouse and others. A pair of eagles nests in the park, and in certain years it chooses the most impressive trees in order to raise its young. Vegetation is strongly influenced by soil, altitude and exposure. At higher altitude we have vineyards and hazel woods of oak and chestnut trees, then around 2000 meters the beech forest - here at the southern limit of its range – and the endemic Etna birch. This plant lives only here, and it differs from more common *Betula pendula* because of smooth, white bark. In particular, the Etna birch lives on the lava land of the eastern slopes of the volcano at an altitude between 1300 and 2100 meters. Higher up the trees disappear, leaving room for shrubs and *pulvini* of plants such as *Astragalus sp.*, *Senecius sp.* and others. The park covers over 58,000 hectares in the province of Catania.

The itinerary
Certainly one of the most interesting of the paths proposed and marked by the park, this trail is on the north-east of the volcano. Access is from the Citelli refuge, easily reached by the road that

goes from Linguaglossa or from Fornazzo. The departure point is from a track closed to vehicular traffic by a barrier, just before arriving at the refuge. We walk through the rare and beautiful birch wood of the endemic *Betula aetnensis*. Beyond a small stone building - a pen with drinking trough - and following yellow poles, you leave the track and turn right along a path that goes down into the wood now becoming increasingly dense. This is the most beautiful stretch of the route, as it passes through the ancient lava flow of 1865 that - during a massive eruption lasted five months - gave rise, among other things, to the seven eruptive cones of the hills of Sartorius, named after the German scholar Sartorius von Waltershausen, among the first to chart the principal eruptions of Etna. You walk on beautiful black sand which covers a layer of lava on average about twelve metres deep, between young pine and larch and Etna broom. With a bit of luck and attention you can see some of the animals that frequent this region, including kestrels, magpies and wild rabbits.

On the ground grow many plants of great interest to botanists, such as chamomile and Etna romice. Particularly abundant and showy are the pink cushions of the beautiful Etna *Saponaria*, whose roots were formerly used for washing clothes in the village built on the slopes of *muntagna*. From here it's quick to return the way you came, along the path to the refuge of Citelli, about an hour and a half in all.

Internet
www.parcoetna.it

Sicily / Zingaro Nature Reserve

THE PATH OF THE PALMS

Among the most important and spectacular nature reserves in Sicily, the Zingaro Reserve protects part of the north-west coast of the island. It is a rocky coast, characterized by high limestone cliffs that plunge into the sea between sandy coves, caves and ravines. The altitudes range from sea level to the 913 meters of Mount Speziale. Despite the rugged morphology and the pronounced differences in height, the area was cultivated until only a few decades ago.

Where
The nature reserve of the Zingaro is the first in Sicily, extending 1,658 hectares and created in 1981 in the wake of a popular uprising to oppose the construction of yet another coastal road close to Trapani, towards the promontory of San Vito Lo Capo. The municipalities involved are Castellammare del Golfo and San Vito lo Capo, both in the province of Trapani. Today it can still be reached from the south on foot, starting from a tunnel which was intended to be a road. The gaping wound cut into the mountain from the early works (later suspended) on the north side, as well as being a gash visible in the distance, also serves as a warning.

The itinerary
From Scopello, not far from Castellammare del Golfo (motorway exit Trapani-Palermo), we reach the car park south of the reserve at a kiosk where you pay an entrance fee (please note, dogs are not allowed, even on a leash). A walk along the path that we suggest is the so-called coastal path, (there is another half way up and then a high one leading to the high limestone cliffs that almost vertically reach 913 meters), which winds through seven

kilometres of beautiful, almost entirely untouched coastline. It is very pleasant and not particularly difficult. There are many views on the cliffs and coves to remember, walking through carob and columns of flowering agave. But the symbolic species among the plants of the protected area is without doubt the Dwarf Palm or European Fan Palm (*Chamaerops humilis*), the only palm to grow spontaneously in the Mediterranean, which is present here with a singular abundance. In fact, the large number of palm trees and even their size can be explained by past cultivation; they were used for packaging of many everyday items such as bags, brooms, hats, and fans to stir the fire which were lit with the leaves.

As for the animals, the most coveted sight is the rare Bonelli's eagle (*Hieraaetus fasciatus*), a pair of which nest on the walls of the reserve, but you need to crane your neck and be very lucky. Peregrine falcons, kestrels and buzzards also live here, while turning your binoculars out to sea you can often identify the outlines of the major and minor shearwaters chasing the waves. Moving from cala del Varo, cala della 'Disa, cala Berretta and cala Marinella you reach the contrada Uzzo, where you can visit a Museum of Farming and where there is a picnic area and water supply. To return, simply retrace your steps, although for the most intrepid walker there is also a museum of maritime activities to visit at the north entrance, at San Vito Lo Capo. Calculate a round trip journey of only about two and a half hours.

Internet
www.riservazingaro.it

advertising

Tuscany
PODERE BELLAVISTA

A must for nature lovers, a renovated stone farmhouse with private pool in secluded grounds, surrounded by 12 hectares of land is truly idyllic. Undiscovered, unspoiled Maremma hills behind Grosseto - area rich in wildlife, birds, butterflies, wild flowers.
Location: Roccalbegna, Grosseto area
Nearest airport: Pisa at 178 Kilometres

www.holiday-rentals.co.uk/p61650

www.ingramcontent.com/pod-product-compliance
Lightning Source LLC
Chambersburg PA
CBHW071700040426
42446CB00011B/1851